OPPOSING AMBITIONS

SHERRYL KLEINMAN

Opposing
AMBITIONS

GENDER AND IDENTITY IN AN
ALTERNATIVE ORGANIZATION

THE UNIVERSITY OF CHICAGO PRESS
Chicago & London

SHERRYL KLEINMAN is professor of sociology at the University of North Carolina, Chapel Hill. She is the author of *Equals before God: Seminarians as Humanistic Professionals* (1984) and coauthor of *Emotions and Fieldwork* (1993).

The University of Chicago Press, Chicago 60637
The University of Chicago Press, Ltd., London
©1996 by Sherryl Kleinman
All rights reserved. Published 1996
Printed in the United States of America
05 04 03 02 01 00 99 98 97 96   1 2 3 4 5
ISBN: 0-226-44004-4 (cloth)
        0-226-44005-2 (paper)

Library of Congress Cataloging-in-Publication Data

Kleinman, Sherryl.
    Opposing ambitions : gender and identity in an alternative organization /
Sherryl Kleinman.
        p.   cm.
    Includes bibliographical references and index.
    1. Organizational behavior—United States—Case studies.   2. Business
anthropology—United States—Case studies.   3. Corporate culture—
United States—Case studies.   4. Subculture—United States—Case
studies.   5. Medical centers—North Carolina—Chapel Hill—
Management—Case studies.   6. Sex discrimination in employment—
United States—Case studies.   7. Discrimination in employment—
United States—Case studies.   I. Title.
HD58.7.K564   1996
302.3'5—dc20   95-35972
                                                                        CIP

CONTENTS

ACKNOWLEDGMENTS

MANY PEOPLE STUCK WITH ME THROUGH THE LONG HAUL OF this project. Barbara Stenross, the friend I talked to first about this project, heard years of whining and occasional joy, talked with me about the fieldwork and the findings, and read more drafts of thought-pieces and chapters than I (or she) can remember. When my spirits sagged, she told me, "This is a complicated story, so it'll take time."

Martha McMahon, a friend since our year in the MA program at McMaster University, read drafts of chapters, talked with me through email and expensive phone calls when I ran into snags, and demanded that I finish this story "because it's important." She made me especially aware of similarities between my analysis of this small organization and other progressive movements and organizations. Much of chapter 6, where I move beyond the organization I studied, is a product of her pushing.

Barbara Rauschenbach, a friend since my graduate school days at the University of Minnesota, heard about this project through visits to Ithaca, letters, phone calls, and email. At a moment when I thought of abandoning the writing, she said, "You have to finish this book because I want to know how the story ends!" I couldn't let her down.

Several years ago I thought I would write, "I'd like to thank Michael Schwalbe for putting up with my silence about this project." When we met, I was hesitant to talk about a project that was already taking "too long." The good news is also the bad news; once I started talking about the book, I wouldn't shut up. Michael lived with this project, made comments on drafts, and provided daily support. His questions and insights gave me more work to do, but strengthened the story in ways I could not have anticipated. Our loving partnership sustained me through the revisions.

I am grateful to the members of my writing group: Jane Brown, Marcy Lansman, and Fabienne Worth. They heard me read parts of the manuscript weekly for over four years, offered comments, supported me through down times, and shared lots of laughter.

My mother, Bella Kleinman, wanted me to complete this project even more than I did and kept repeating, "You've really got to finish that book." The mantra finally worked.

Many people read parts of the manuscript and supported me in all kinds of ways: Howard Aldrich, Howard Becker, Leandra Bedini, Nicole Biggart, Patricia Bryan, Sally Boyd, Candace Clark, Martha Copp, Arlene Kaplan Daniels, Eric Dishman, Carolyn Ellis, Gary Alan Fine, Mary Gallant, Karla Henderson, Arlie Hochschild, Lori Hoyt, Lyn Lofland, Julie Manushkin, Judith Meece, Douglas Mitchell, Shulamit Reinharz, Erica Rothman, Allan Schnaiberg, Mary Sheriff, Barbara Smalley, Bev Wiggins, Jim Wiggins, and Jacqueline Wiseman.

I had one semester's leave through the University of North Carolina, Chapel Hill, to work on this project. I also spent a summer at the Institute for the Arts and Humanities on UNC's campus, and had a Spencer grant for another summer.

The people at Renewal gave generously of their time and patience. Although the organization, in the incarnation I studied it, no longer exists, I hope that former members find something of value to take with them as they continue to participate in alternative work.

I dedicate this book to the friends of writers, those people who nurture, cajole, and push us when we need it.

one

INTRODUCTION

IN JUNE OF 1980 I DEFENDED MY DISSERTATION AT THE UNIversity of Minnesota and promptly got sick. My symptoms persisted, and I endured some unpleasant medical tests. The test results were negative, but I still felt sick. In early August, a young male resident with a ponytail examined me and said, "Everything seems normal. So what is going on in your life?" His question surprised me, and I blurted out, "There's this job I've taken and I have to move across the country." He asked me how I felt about the job, and after I told him he said, "You sound ambivalent about moving. Either call your new boss right now and say you won't take the job, or get on a plane." These stark options cleared the haze that had surrounded me for six weeks. I made my reservations the next day.

I moved to my new home and my first job, where I became an assistant professor of sociology. Faculty members at Minnesota beamed when they heard I'd gotten this job. I'd seen those expressions before—on the faces of my family members when they heard that a young woman was going to marry a "professional man." At twenty-seven I'd managed to find the career equivalent of the good catch.

Even so, I was depressed. I'd wrenched myself out of a city I liked, left a community of friends who had the good sense to stretch out the time it took them to finish their dissertations, and given up the satisfying position of the good student whom faculty treat as an honorary colleague. My own Golden Age was behind me.

I also felt ambivalent about taking on the role of professor. Professors—even untenured ones—profess. We should know more than others, impress our students, and publish without having to ask for help from others, especially from those who will later decide if our work is worthy of tenure. These expectations violated my antielitist attitudes. Like many of my generation I scorned elitism and felt the most comfortable in relationships that mirrored good friendships. It was easy to have personal, peerlike relations as an undergraduate and then as a graduate student. Students, at least during the 1970s, were supposed to dress down, act informally, and make mistakes. I thought I now had to think and talk and look and act in ways that set me apart from students, which in my case meant my good friends. It was time to throw out those old jeans.

But I didn't. Instead, I remained caught between two worlds (actually, several). I was a qualitative researcher in a largely quantitative department, one of two women in a department of men, and a person who identified with the informality of the sixties but now lived in the more formal eighties.

For my dissertation I had studied the dilemmas of professional socialization experienced by ministry students in a nontraditional seminary (Kleinman 1984). What would I study next? I found myself noticing flyers for alternative organizations, including a women's center and an alternative magazine. At a health food restaurant I picked up a free newsletter from Renewal (a pseudonym), an alternative health organization. Here's what I read:

> Our approach is "wholistic." This means that we encourage the acceptance, nurturing and integration of all aspects of the individual: mental, physical, emotional, spiritual and social. We believe that optimal health can be attained only by viewing the person as a whole and by emphasizing that the locus of responsibility for achieving such "wholeness" lies with each individual.

Well before I had talked to the young resident at the University of Minnesota, I suspected that there were connections between the mind and the body, or at least *my* mind and *my* body. So, I decided to look into Renewal as a research site. One October afternoon I found my way to an old, slightly rundown two-story house. I was pleased that Renewal had the look of an alternative organization—homey and funky.

I met two participants that day, both of whom, I learned later, were core actors at Renewal. Carla, a staff member and volunteer, had just been appointed Coordinator (note: all names are pseudonyms). She was in the "office area" on the main floor, doing something with the membership list. Karen, who I later learned was a novice practitioner, emerged from the bathroom, towel-drying her hair. I had mixed reactions to this scene. I enjoyed the casual atmosphere, but Karen's behavior gave me a twinge; I found it *too* casual. I quickly suppressed my reaction since I thought of myself as someone who appreciated informality. I told myself that she acted this way because she thought clients weren't around.

Where *were* the clients? That worried me, too. I didn't see anyone waiting for a practitioner. Perhaps a few clients were upstairs, I told myself. (Carla had said that's where the practitioners treated clients.) But I didn't hear any noises. I kept my doubts to myself.

I asked Carla and Karen how participants might feel about having a sociologist hang around. Both of them thought participants would like the idea. Carla said I'd need the approval of the Board of Directors and suggested I attend the board meeting that evening. At the mention of "board meeting," Karen sighed and said, "Oh, you might be bored. We talk so much about money!" Carla urged me to study Renewal, saying they needed someone "who'd be objective" about the organization. At the time I thought it an odd choice of words.

Later that evening I attended my first board meeting (these were held every other week for about three hours). All twelve members were there—half women and half men. They were white, mostly in their late twenties or early thirties. Some of the men had long hair and wore jeans and tie-dyed shirts. Some of the women wore peasant skirts. I felt pretty comfortable, though I had the vague sense that I was in another time. Yet the content of the meeting jarred with members' personae. Much of the talk was about budgets, money, fundraisers, and the like. I remembered Karen's warning: Would this study bore me? No one talked about holistic healing, countercultural ideals, or relationships among members.

Board members' talk, though not their appearance, contradicted my assumptions about "alternative organizations." I expected members to talk about the interesting stuff, not the kinds of things that I imagined board members in conventional organizations talked about. At the same time I wondered if Renewal would stay in operation. Their references to being "in the red" left me feeling anxious about whether the organization would fold before I had a chance to study it.

By the end of the evening I felt ambivalent about the study, the organization, and the participants. My reactions to Renewal alternated throughout the study. Sometimes I thought it wasn't alternative enough, a reaction I had after listening to hours of money-talk at that first meeting. Was members' idealism limited to their clothing? Other times I thought of members as disorganized or as acting inappropriately for a health organization. Hence my discomfort at watching Karen drying her hair in the public space of Renewal. Renewal seemed neither a legitimate conventional organization nor a convincing alternative. As I wrote in my fieldnotes, "Renewal isn't even a legitimate illegitimate organization!"

I felt guilty about my conflicted feelings toward participants. Fieldworkers are supposed to like those who are nice enough to let us in. The first lesson of fieldwork—perhaps the main one—is to develop empathy. But through the long process of this study I learned, then wrote about (see Kleinman and Copp 1993), a different methodological lesson: what researchers feel is much less important than how we use those feelings to understand the people we study. The complex feelings I experienced throughout the research and writing of this book eventually became resources for analyzing the data.

Examining my ambivalence about Renewal and about my first job gave me insights into *participants'* struggles. Like them, I was someone who had experienced the late sixties and the seventies as a period of self-transformation. Those of us who identified with that period thought of our earlier experiences as a time when we questioned conventional authority and tried to live out egalitarian personal relations. Although most of us didn't have a label for who we had been during the sixties (though a few members of Renewal considered themselves ex-hippies), that era continued to be a reference point for who we were or had become.

This nameless identity—which I will call "alternative"—was a *moral identity*. By this I mean an identity that people invest with moral significance; our belief in ourselves as good people depends on whether we think our actions and reactions are consistent with that identity. By this definition, any identity that testifies to a person's good character can be a moral identity, such as mother, Christian, breadwinner, or feminist. (For other sociological uses of the term "moral" see Goffman 1961:125–69; Katz 1975.) In the case of Renewal, participants felt good about themselves as long as they believed that their experiences of the sixties and seventies continued to inform their lives, especially their collective work at Renewal.

For participants, the worth of Renewal and their worth as individuals depended on whether they believed they were "doing something different," a phrase I heard repeatedly throughout the research. But there were other, contradictory meanings of self that participants cared about. Like many white, middle-class, college-educated people in their late twenties and early thirties in 1980, participants also wanted to be seen, and to see themselves, as mature, responsible, and professional. In the late 1970s and throughout the eighties, the media portrayed "the sixties" as a time of youthful idealism, drugs, and rock 'n' roll. Movies like *The Big Chill* and newspaper articles about yuppies mocked the sixties as a fad, a period of adolescence.

Understandably, then, members of Renewal wanted to distance themselves from these images. I too learned that studying an alternative organization had costs. Shortly after I started the study, one usually open-minded sociologist said he thought it was time for researchers to study "normal organizations." Others kidded me about the "flaky place" I was studying when all I had said were the words "holistic health." I was told that a university committee had turned down my application for a small grant because members assumed that Renewal was a "fly-by-night organization." Carla's statement about wanting someone "objective" to study Renewal started to make sense. Ironically, having me around—the ambivalent, newly minted professor/sociologist—might help participants feel legitimate.

Thus, members of Renewal faced a different dilemma from those who participated in more radically alternative organizations of the late sixties (Rothschild and Whitt 1986). At that time, participants in free schools (Swidler 1979), hot lines (Mansbridge 1980), communes (Berger 1981), food co-ops (Reinharz 1983), free clinics, and law collectives (Rothschild and Whitt 1986; Case and Taylor 1979) rejected conventional authority and underwent mutual and self-criticism (Rothschild and Whitt 1986) to live up to egalitarian ideals. Members of Renewal—which opened its doors in 1978—wanted a *legitimate* alternative.

The twofold structure of the organization mirrored members' dual concerns. One part of Renewal was constituted by six private practitioners (their word) who were paid by individual clients and then gave a portion of their earnings (determined by the board) to the organization. This payment was sometimes referred to as rent. The other, "educational," part of Renewal was nonprofit and was run by three or four staff members and several volunteers. Low-cost classes and workshops were offered to the public through this part of Renewal. Staff did the office work for Renewal, ran the physical plant, and were responsible for putting the membership bulletin together. They also helped produce the newsletter that announced classes. Practitioners received about thirty dollars an hour for their services as psychotherapists, nutrition therapists, massage practitioners, or stress managers. Given Renewal's financial problems, staff were often unpaid, and received four dollars an hour when they did get paid. Overlap existed between the two parts of the organization; practitioners did some volunteer work, often headed major committees, and sometimes taught workshops. Staff, volunteers, and practitioners were represented on the board.

I felt uneasy about the structure because it seemed inequitable and entirely conventional. Weren't members perpetuating a two-class system at Renewal? In addition to discrepancies in pay between staff and practitioners, staff members sometimes made appointments for the practitioners or gave them phone messages. Although staff were presumably working for the nonprofit part of

Renewal, they were, to some extent, working for private practitioners but not getting paid for their services.

Although I was initially concerned about inequities in pay, I eventually became more upset by differences in power, prestige, and respect. Two male practitioners, the only remaining founding members of Renewal, had the greatest influence, particularly at board meetings. (A third founding member, also a male practitioner, quit the organization a few months after I arrived.) Jack was Chair of the Board of Directors. Ron headed the committee that determined all classes and workshops. Since the board made most decisions, from hiring and firing to approving all committee work, having influence on the board was no small matter. In addition, participants accorded Ron and Jack the most respect, attention, nurturance, and affection.

Why did they enjoy such esteem? Because they had started the organization, participants regarded them as "the pioneers," as one staff member put it, and hence those most committed to holistic healing. At the same time, others thought of Ron and Jack as organized, responsible, and competent. As those who symbolized the alternative vision, yet lived it out through such conventionally high-status positions as Chair of the Board and Chair of the Program Committee, Jack and Ron helped reinforce members' belief that Renewal was an alternative, yet serious, organization.

One might argue that these practitioners deserved the recognition they got and that my suspicions about their greater rewards were unwarranted. Was I inappropriately holding up Renewal to the standards of alternative organizations from the sixties? Every time I reread a draft of a chapter I worried that I was being judgmental rather than sociological. Did I have to examine how members failed to live up to their alternative ideals? This feeling, like my ambivalence, helped me analyze the data because it led me to ask: what are *participants'* ideas about equality? Perhaps I'd discover that Ron's and Jack's elevated status made sense.

I learned that participants' notions of equality were individualistic and apolitical, almost antipolitical. For them, occupational status, gender, income, and so on were unimportant; these social attributes constituted superficial differences among people. They believed that each individual is unique, special, and worthy of equal respect. But my observations revealed that members gave each other *un*equal respect and that respect depended in large part on participants' social statuses. Hence, they failed to live up to their own standards. This was an important *sociological* observation.

Opposing Ambitions is a story about identity and about inequality. Here I tell how members sustained discordant images of themselves as both alternative and legitimate by not recognizing the ways in which they were conventional. Members denied that they *cared* about feeling legitimate while using conventional bureaucratic rhetoric to make them feel that their work at Renewal, and Renewal itself, were legitimate. Most importantly, members failed to see how their attempts to meet their conflicting identity needs led them to treat each other unequally and thus contradict their own ideals.

Inequalities at Renewal were gendered. This was true beyond the obvious difference in pay between the mostly male group of practitioners and the all-female staff and volunteers. Members had conventional ideas about gender and authority which underlay their unequal treatment of each other. Because "real professionals" were presumed to be male, the female practitioners couldn't provide members with the same degree of conventional legitimacy as their male counterparts. The men's gender, then, became a resource for bringing legitimacy to the organization and to themselves.

Members' claim to an alternative identity was grounded in their belief that they were making sacrifices for the cause of holistic health. Because participants assumed that the male practitioners—like other bright, white, middle-class men—*could have* pursued lucrative, prestigious careers, they defined the male practitioners as those who had made sacrifices to work for an alternative cause. Board members and staff were wary of the female practitioners; they thought of these women as having *sought* privileges (through education and careers) rather than having given them up.

Understanding the relationship between gender, privilege, and the alternative identity can also explain why participants didn't define the staff members' actions as sacrifices. In addition to taking care of Renewal and those within it, the staff members who were in charge of paying the bills often paid the rent and utilities instead of themselves. But, like the housewives that Viviana Zelizer

(1989:365) studied, the staff women's money "retained a collective identity, while men's . . . money was differentiated and individualized." Since members expected the staff women, as the "housewives" of the organization, to give without receiving "individual" payment, members didn't define the staff's unpaid work as a sacrifice. Yet, when practitioners said they'd pay more rent to Renewal, others expressed gratitude. Thus, members' "economy of gratitude" (Hochschild 1989) reflected conventional gender expectations. As Arlie Hochschild (1989:95) has argued, "the broader culture helps fix in the individual a mental baseline against which any action or object seems extra, and so, like a gift." Only those who had privileges to sacrifice—the male practitioners—could get points for giving them up.

Members claimed that money was a tainted substance and that having to deal with money matters was either distasteful or, as Karen put it, "boring." Yet I discovered that money, and members' endless talk about it, usually made them feel good. Participants talked about money in ways that bolstered their *alternative* identity. At the same time, talking about money made them feel they were engaged in serious business and hence weren't flaky. In chapter 2, I will show how participants used money symbolically.

Members supposedly rejected signs of conventionality, but they adopted many features of bureaucratic organizations: titles, committee reports, detailed minutes of meetings, and so on. Yet having these signs of organizational legitimacy failed to undermine their sense of themselves as alternative. In chapter 3, I show how members took signs of conventionality and used them as indicators of their commitment to the alternative cause. I also show how their ideas about equality and about gender reinforced the authority of those who held higher positions in the organization.

Members reinforced their moral identity at their retreats. There, they concentrated on their relationships with each other through acts of communion (e.g., handholding, hugs, and circles) and acts of confrontation (e.g., talking about their angry feelings toward each other). Chapter 4 shows how their vocabulary of emotions made it difficult for members to recognize or to talk about social or political inequalities. Ironically, their "feminine" language failed to empower the women who held low-status positions, but instead empowered the already privileged men.

CHAPTER ONE

Given the inequalities at Renewal, why did the women join the staff or become volunteers? Chapter 5 examines how they came to participate, changes in their perspective over time, and their eventual disillusionment. These women entered the organization with a strong commitment to alternative ideals; they shared what Carol Gilligan (1982) calls an "ethic of care." By the time they left the organization, the women believed that others, particularly Ron and Jack, had taken advantage of their selflessness. They quit Renewal with an ambivalent attitude toward alternative organizations.

I attended board meetings from October 1980 to December 1981. I arrived early to talk with board members before the meetings, and often stayed afterwards. I took detailed notes (as close to verbatim as possible), which I typed up the following day. I attended all retreats, often attended practitioners' biweekly meetings, participated in most fund-raisers, and went to workshops on holistic healing. I conducted two-hour, tape-recorded interviews (some lasted longer) from 1982 to 1985 with twelve central members. I also examined organizational documents, including minutes of board meetings, newsletters, membership bulletins, and financial and other committee reports.

My analysis of Renewal is developed from a symbolic interactionist perspective (Mead 1934; Blumer 1969). From this perspective, every action, whether mundane or dramatic, has meaning for those who engage in it. Hence we cannot understand the world that participants share unless we know their perspective. Qualitative research practices—watching, listening, asking questions, reading what participants write, talking to them at length—provide the means for understanding what participants think, feel, say, or do (Lofland and Lofland 1984). In this study I learned also to pay attention to what participants kept out of their consciousness, which emotions were taboo, what they didn't talk about, and what they refrained from doing. A patterned silence, while sometimes hard to notice, has as much significance as a repetitive noise (Olesen and Whittaker 1968; Smith and Kleinman 1989).

This book differs from traditional qualitative accounts by offering a "critical ethnography" (Thomas 1993). I discuss the political consequences of participants' meanings and the "constraints that give some groups or individuals unfair advantage to the disadvantage of others" (Thomas 1993:5; see also Agger 1991). As a feminist, I was committed to figuring out how those who saw themselves as alternative managed to reproduce conventional gender inequalities (Flax 1987; Jaggar 1989). In chapters 2 through 5, I stay close to the data, telling the intersecting stories of identity and inequality at Renewal. Chapter 6 explores the significance of the study for understanding how identity needs and gender shape behavior in both conventional and alternative organizations. At Renewal, members' strong investment in their moral identity kept them from seeing how their behaviors contradicted their ideals. In chapter 6 I discuss how this failure of perception occurs in other contexts, and how the case of Renewal can help us understand how moral identities impede or foster social change more generally. I also show how the case of Renewal can illuminate the process whereby taken-for-granted gender inequalities undermine efforts to create egalitarian work organizations and social movement organizations.

In looking beyond the organization I studied I came to see that many of us are caught in the same kinds of contradictions present at Renewal. Whether we call ourselves feminists, radicals, or progressives, we too at times deny that we act in ways that subvert our noblest principles, because doing so preserves a cherished moral identity. We become so invested in our belief in ourselves as radicals or "good people" that we cannot see the reactionary or hurtful consequences of our behaviors. I urge readers, then, to look for parallels between their own experiences and those of the people at Renewal. Like many of us, they tried to live out an alternative, yet could not avoid reproducing conventional inequalities.

two

MONEY AS MORAL CURRENCY

IN A CAPITALIST SOCIETY, "MONEY IS OFTEN EQUATED WITH goodness, ability, talent, drive, even moral uprightness" (Blumstein and Schwartz 1983:69). We may criticize how people spend their money, especially the conspicuous consumption of the nouveau riche, but making money is something we expect adults to do. Poor kids and rich kids know this, though they have different expectations about the likelihood that they'll succeed (Sennett and Cobb 1972). Not making enough money, particularly for men in this society, often indicates to others a failure of character (Liebow 1967; Newman 1988). This isn't surprising in a society in which people believe that upward mobility is a real and likely possibility for those who work hard enough.

Yet along with the idea that money brings prestige and even happiness is the notion that money corrupts and poverty builds character. Some upper–middle class parents worry about spoiling their children and make them work for their allowance or get jobs to pay for their cars. Popular sitcoms, such as *Good Times*, depict poor black families as happy despite their poverty. The TV version of poverty says: they ain't got money, but they got love.

Although participants in the youth movements of the 1960s and 1970s might have seen through the romanticized portrayal of poverty on television, they nevertheless took to the idea that living with less builds character. Because they hadn't been born into poverty, they couldn't claim that they had struggled and suffered their way to character. But they could do one better—refuse to accept their middle-class privileges. They criticized the consumption of the middle class and rejected careers that might have made them rich. Although disparaged as "slumming" by those who criticized them, some youths chose a lifestyle of simplicity, living in communes (Berger 1981) or in low-rent districts, working in alternative organizations, such as free schools (Swidler 1979), progressive newspapers, or food co-ops (Rothschild and Whitt 1986). Thus, they added a dimension to poverty that built their own moral identity—they *chose* to live with less.

From the countercultural perspective, then, money is tainted and leads to corruption and co-optation. Understandably, then, members at Renewal told me that they disliked talking about money, even though they talked about money-related matters about 90 percent of the time at their board meetings. At first I assumed that they *had to* talk about money. In a capitalist context most organizations, even alternatives, must deal with money. And Renewal had financial problems: when I first came to Renewal I learned that the organization was in the red and owed two staff members two thousand dollars in back pay. Given these stark material conditions, how could they avoid talking about money?

Thus, I initially thought of Renewal's poverty as a social fact and their money-talk as a necessary consequence of their unstable financial position. This chapter turns that analysis on its head: I conceive of poverty—in the case of Renewal—as a social construction rather than as a plain fact. If we understand members' poverty in the light of the identity they desired, it becomes something they *wanted* rather than something imposed on them from the outside. Their alternative identity was based on the idea that they had sacrificed middle-class privileges. Their belief in themselves as alternative actors and as an alternative organization depended on "objective" indicators of financial struggle.

As I will show, members used money—this potentially tainted substance—for their own *moral enhancement*. Their discussions about making money built up their alternative identity. But unlike their predecessors in alternative organizations of the 1960s, members of Renewal also wanted to think of themselves as responsible organizational actors. I will show how their talk about money reinforced their image of themselves as unconventional yet allowed them to feel they were doing the serious work of a conventional organization. This was a difficult feat, because admitting that they cared about conventional legitimacy would have put their alternative identity into question. By believing that they had to talk about money all the time, members masked the fact that they also valued the legitimacy that came from engaging in money-talk.

In addition to living simply, members of nontraditional organizations in the sixties and seventies took the idea of equality, especially with regard to pay, as a serious matter. They rotated tasks and received equal pay for both routine and more interesting work. Members of Renewal, as I described in chapter 1, paid their workers unequally. Also, staff members received their pay from the poor, nonprofit part of the organization and consequently often received no pay. The practitioners were paid directly by their clients and then paid part of their income to Renewal for rent and services.

Given these arrangements, how could members claim an alternative identity? By generating the sense that they had a chronic survival crisis, members maintained the fiction that all of them—practitioners and staff—were *in the same boat*. They believed they shared a mission: fighting to keep Renewal alive despite the conventional environment on the "outside." The solidarity that this crisis produced made it difficult for them to recognize unequal divisions *within* the organization. Hence, their focus on the "survival crisis" masked inequalities in distribution of money within the organization.

Board members discussed three main ways of increasing Renewal's income: raising fees for classes and practitioners' services, having fund-raisers, and hiring a physician. As I will show, their talk about these money matters helped them manage their contradictory identity as a legitimate alternative.

A PHYSICIAN'S REFLECTED GLORY

After long discussions about the current money crisis, someone would say, with a sigh, "Oh, if only we had a physician." Initially, that suggestion surprised me. How did members come to feel that the ultimate solution to their problem was to hire someone from the medical establishment?

Members believed that having a physician would solve their money problems. One board member pointed out that a physician could get clients' services covered through third-party payments. For example, if a physician approved a client's need for massage, then his or her health insurance might cover it. Presumably, more people would become clients at Renewal if their health insurance covered the costs. But since the practitioners only gave a percentage of their earnings to Renewal, a physician's recommendations wouldn't bring in much money.

Having a physician on the board or in practice at Renewal might have added legitimacy to the organization and thus brought in more clients. Then again, those who turned to holistic therapies as a reaction *against* the field of medicine might have assumed that Renewal wasn't alternative enough and gone elsewhere. But members didn't weigh these different hypotheses. Rather, they talked as if a physician would be a cure-all for their financial problems.

I could have concluded that members were inept or unrealistic. But I think they avoided figuring out the details of what a physician would bring to Renewal in dollars because these details were irrelevant for their purposes. Members wanted a physician primarily for *symbolic* reasons—having someone with an MD willing to work at Renewal made them feel they were part of a legitimate health center. Whether a physician attracted or turned off potential clients, members *themselves* wanted some association with a practitioner who had an MD.

Members couldn't have admitted that they cared about the reflected glory that a physician would bring to Renewal because this would have challenged their alternative identity. Board members who suggested hiring a physician always did so with deep sighs, as if to say, "I wish this weren't necessary." But *believing* it was necessary helped them build their alternative identity. "Needing" a physician meant that they were indeed poor and thus an authentic alternative. If they were successful in conventional terms they wouldn't have to rely on a physician—someone in a conventional profession—to help them stay afloat. Thus, members could look for a physician while maintaining an image of themselves as people who questioned the legitimacy of the medical profession.

Members talked at length about the *kind* of person and practice they'd find acceptable from someone with an MD. Not just any physician would do. Such talk made members feel they were engaging in the kind of conversation that should go on in an alternative organization. By turning their desire for a physician into a morally tinged issue they could look for a physician and yet build up their alternative identity in the process.

Participants came in contact with a family physician, Frank Sampson, who first became a board member and later practiced at Renewal about six hours a week:

> At a practitioner meeting Ron said, "This should remain confidential. I don't want people to get all rah-rah about this and then it doesn't work out. But I've just had talks with Frank Sampson and he's interested in becoming more involved with Renewal. He'll be running for the board." Karen and Jack looked pleased. Karen said, "Neat." Ron added, "I value his services a lot, and I think he'd be excellent."

I never heard participants sound as excited over any other potential board member. (Since the turnover rate was high, I heard a lot of talk about people who might join the board.) Members sighed when they talked about needing a physician in the abstract, but displayed only enthusiasm about bringing in Frank Sampson. Here was a physician who thought highly enough of them to be on the board of their alternative center.

Frank had a position of honor at Renewal. One indicator of his high status was the level of excitement generated over his possible board membership. But there was other compelling evidence: members let Frank off the hook for actions they didn't accept from each other. For example, after he was elected, Frank missed the first board meeting. In all cases but Frank's, members treated attendance at meetings as a critical sign of organizational commitment (see chapter 3). Board members always expressed concern about those who missed meetings early on in their tenure. Why someone missed a board meeting mattered; the acceptable excuses I heard included severe illness (not a cold or a chronic backache), a partner losing a child in childbirth, and a parent dying.

What happened in Frank's case? Jack, the Chair of the Board, announced with pride that Frank wasn't at the meeting because he was running in a marathon, "which shows you the kind of person he is." Everyone looked pleased. They understood that Jack's comment meant that Frank was the *right* kind of person for Renewal. Running in a marathon rather than coming to a meeting showed members that Frank was an atypical doctor and thus someone who suited their needs. A *physician* who chose to run in a race rather than attend a business meeting demonstrated appropriate distance from his conventional role. No one else who offered such healthy reasons for missing a meeting was so cheerfully excused.

Frank's membership in a high-status, *conventional* occupation enabled him to occupy a position of honor in an organization whose members prided themselves on being *alternative*. Members thought that Frank's association with Renewal might taint his reputation in the medical community. Hence, they thought of him as taking a risk and making a sacrifice. Soon after he became a board member, Frank worked a few hours a week at Renewal, which members also saw as a sacrifice. Since most members didn't have Frank's "capital," they couldn't give it up and gain special points in the process.

How else might members have reacted to Frank? Since Frank was a physician, members might have put him through extra hoops to prove that he was truly alternative. Or they might have treated his behavior in the same way they treated their own. Yet they did the opposite, complimenting him for acting in ways they disapproved of in each other. We interpret behavior as generous when it comes from people in higher-status positions, as in the case of fathers who do childcare and, because they are male, receive applause for their efforts while mothers do not. If we accepted that status as equal rather than better, then we'd also give that behavior equal weight.

What members *didn't* talk about, even after Frank started practicing part-time at Renewal, was the discrepancy between what physicians and holistic practitioners usually charged for their services. A physician would probably charge for fifteen or twenty minutes what a holistic practitioner charged for an hour or longer. Yet members failed to talk about this matter. In the case of other practitioners, "what to charge" at times became a hot issue, as I discuss in the next section. A holistic practitioner had to justify that his or her service was worth a big fee, but a physician did not. Members' unacknowledged sense that a serious health organization must have a physician was so strong that they failed to recognize the different standards they judged him by.

Members found in Frank a person who could make them feel legitimate without them having to recognize that they cared about his legitimacy. By playing up the ways that Frank violated the stereotype of the physician, they convinced themselves that they weren't hiring a typical doctor, but a holistic healer who happened to have an MD. Thus, they were acting as responsible *alternative* actors. Yet Frank the "un-physician" still had an MD, a family practice outside Renewal, and a university affiliation. Thus, he could make them feel they were members of a *legitimate* health center by his willingness to support them. In this convoluted fashion, hiring someone from the very profession members were distinguishing their services from became the best solution to their problems of identity.

MONEY-TALK AS MORAL CURRENCY

Members often talked about raising fees for classes, workshops, and practitioners' services or increasing membership dues. Board members were ambivalent about raising fees, particularly for classes and practitioners' services. For example, at one board meeting

> Someone mentioned fee hikes. Karen (practitioner) said, "I don't know about that. I think we'll put clients off that way." Bob said, "Look, we need to do this to survive. Everything's inflated these days, and our fees should come up, too." Carla (staff) said, "I don't know. I don't want us to become another middle-class commodity." Manny (practitioner) said, "But we'll still use a sliding scale."

This discussion was typical. Members always talked about whether *any* raise in fees was morally acceptable. After much talk, they'd agree to increase their fees. This then led to a long negotiation about the acceptability of a particular amount. Members spent hours considering whether a small increase in charges for services—even one dollar—was acceptable. Occasionally, members spent so much time agonizing over the raise that they'd discover only much later in the evening that the increase would bring in a negligible amount of money and thus wouldn't get them through their immediate financial problem.

For example, after two hours of discussion about a raise in workshop fees, Bob pointed out that since workshop leaders get 65 percent of the fees (and the rest goes to Renewal), raising fees the proposed amount would bring in only a small amount of money. Similarly, allowing clients to "work off" their class fees by volunteering (proposed as a way to offset increases in fees) also didn't increase Renewal's income. Nor did a sliding scale, which someone always proposed. Yet members talked about such proposals at length and usually adopted them.

For a few months, I felt uneasy, anxious, and frustrated during these discussions. Surely members could come up with a better solution to this chronic financial crisis. But the board members didn't feel as I did. As I listened to their voices, scrutinized their faces, and watched them make points with their hands, they seemed anything *but* bored, uncomfortable, or exasperated. This surprised me: hadn't Karen told me, that first day, that their discussions about money bored her? Yet Karen, along with the others, seemed fully *engaged* in the process. Members looked tired, but not dispirited, by the end of board meetings. Rather, they showed the kind of fatigue that follows meaningful, hard work rather than repetitive, alienated labor.

How could members approach each discussion with renewed vigor? Couldn't they see that their discussions were patterned and predictable? It took me a long time to figure out that members' talk about money had *value*. By talking about money as a moral issue, worrying about whether they had compromised their principles, and finding temporary solutions to their immediate problem, they felt they were doing what members of alternative organizations are supposed to do. *I* found their discussions frustrating, and eventually routine, because I wasn't a member, I didn't participate in the discussions, and thus I couldn't reap the (moral) identity benefits of such talk.

Members' organizational poverty ennobled them. Although no one spoke these words, their endless discussions seemed to say: "The fact that we always need money to stay alive means that we must be doing something right. If we were making a profit, that could mean we'd sold out." As I argued earlier, members' moral identity hinged on their belief that they had sacrificed conventional middle-class privileges, especially money, to work for a cause. Their ongoing financial crisis proved to them that they were indeed an alternative; they *continued* to sacrifice middle-class financial stability.

What if they had treated money as a neutral object? Then they would have asked these questions: How much should we raise fees to get the money we need? How much will people pay? What is the market out there? But such questions would have robbed participants of a source of their esteem as members of an alternative organization—their belief that they are something *more* than a regular establishment.

Although members didn't purposely keep Renewal in debt, their financial problems made it necessary for them to talk often about their plight, to seek "solutions," and thus to have further discussion about the morality of making money. Members' poverty, then, was functional. If they had solved their financial problems, they would have exhausted a resource for maintaining their alternative identity.

There were rules for talking about money. You could only suggest raising fees a small amount; suggesting a big increase meant that you had ignored the needs of the poor. (In addition, by raising fees only a little, they failed to solve their problem and found themselves talking about another raise not long afterwards, thus ensuring more moral negotiation.) You had to express ambivalence about the raise; sounding neutral meant that you didn't care about the poor. You also had to suggest alternative forms of payment, such as volunteering at Renewal. Finally, if you proposed an increase in your rates as a practitioner, you were also expected to discuss the implications of the raise for the collective.

When someone broke a rule, others jumped in to correct him

or her. Intermittent rule-breaking seemed only to reinforce their alternative identity because it heated up the discussion. What happened when a member challenged the belief that lay at the core of their identity—that it was important to sacrifice middle-class privileges? I saw the centrality of poverty to their moral identity when Manny, a well-respected practitioner and one of the three remaining founders of Renewal, broke the rules. For a few months, Manny had expressed an interest in making more money as a practitioner. After missing several practitioner meetings, Manny turned up with the following announcement:

> "I'm raising my rates to forty-five dollars a session [from thirty dollars a session]. I'll still have a sliding scale—I don't turn anyone away—but my base rate will be forty-five dollars." . . . Jack looked upset and said, "I have problems with the inflated rates of psychotherapists. Also, that's a big jump in rate." Karen said, "I feel uncomfortable having anyone charge that much for what we're trying to do." Manny replied, "I don't think poverty consciousness is the way to go." Ron said, "The other side is greed."

Manny announced rather than requested a fee hike, something that upset others. He saved face a little by saying that he would use a sliding scale and "wouldn't turn anyone away." Claiming that he was worth forty-five dollars (while other practitioners charged up to thirty-five dollars) suggested to the other practitioners that he thought his service, which was similar to Jack's, was worth more. Although the gap in pay between staff and practitioners shows that members had conventional ideas about which jobs deserve more money, no one was supposed to hint at the connection between individual worth and money.

Others bristled when he said, "I don't think poverty consciousness is the way to go." He explained that he wanted more financial stability in his life and wanted to buy a house. He made his statements clearly, directly, and in an even tone; he neither apologized for his change of heart nor tried to convince others to feel the same way. His lack of angst and passion also violated one of the board members' rules: you couldn't be matter-of-fact about money. Neutrality in tone meant coldness in heart.

The practitioners came down hard on Manny. They did so for

two reasons. First, he questioned the basis of their alternative identity by rejecting chosen poverty (what he called "poverty consciousness"). Second, Manny also threatened the other, hidden part of their identity—members' desire to see themselves as responsible organizational actors. For example, at an earlier meeting, when the practitioners talked about filling vacancies on the board, Manny said, "I think we should get consumers on the board. If we still need people who set up Renewal to work on the board then I think it's stillborn." His statement shocked members. At another meeting, he said that an organization that couldn't pay its staff was "dead."

Manny intimated that Renewal's financial problems were a product of members' organizational ineptness rather than their lofty ideals. He more than hinted that Renewal was a bogus alternative *and* an ineffective organization. Thus, he made it difficult for members to claim either frame of reference. Despite Manny's popularity and his high status as a practitioner and founder of Renewal, he became too big a threat to members' self-images.

The practitioners discussed Manny's proposal with each other and with board members informally over the next two weeks. Consistent with their discussions about all raises, they discussed whether Manny's proposal would challenge Renewal's identity as an alternative, especially if all the practitioners charged similar fees. Manny failed to show up at the next practitioner meeting. Ron had this to say:

> Two weeks ago when this came up I thought it was only Manny's business. I've given it a lot of thought and talked to a number of people in Renewal and in the community, and now I feel differently. I *do* want to have some input into this and to do what's moral . . . I think there are a number of reasons for not letting him increase his fees. The first is that this decision affects me, us, our image. Second, it's a big increase, a big jump. Third, most of his clients can't afford it, like maybe 80 percent of them. Personally, I feel he's doing it for status reasons, status quo reasons . . . Phew! I said it. That's how I feel.

More discussion followed. Jack said:

If we approve Manny's raise, then I'll have a problem with my own professional identity. On the one hand, it's none of our business. On the other, Manny isn't here, and he didn't call to say he wouldn't be here. I think that's indicative of his participation. I don't support the raise.

Manny quit working at Renewal soon after that. The practitioners reported to the board what had happened. This incident gave practitioners the opportunity to prove to other board members that their commitment to alternative ideals was more important than keeping "one of their own." The practitioners *didn't* tell other board members about their worry, expressed at practitioner meetings, that if Manny charged considerably more than they did, then clients might assume that his services were better than theirs. They also failed to mention that their clients probably wouldn't pay forty-five dollars for their services. As Ron had said, "charging that much would run me out of business."

I don't think the practitioners purposely omitted these concerns. But if the practitioners had revealed their concerns about losing clients or denting their professional reputations, other board members might have seen them as self-interested or insecure.

The practitioners, by focusing mostly on Manny's violation of alternative ideals, reinforced their moral identity and showed that they were committed to resisting conventionality. By bringing select elements of the incident to the board and giving their conclusion—to refuse the raise—the practitioners built solidarity with other board members, and maintained those members' trust in them. The discussion of the event at the board meeting reinforced board members' image of themselves, and the organization, as alternative. Because members defined what had transpired as a crisis that involved an agonizing decision, their actions became an opportunity for *moral renewal*.

We have seen, then, that members framed money-talk in ways that made them feel they were an authentic alternative. In the case of raising fees for services, it is more difficult to provide evidence for my second argument—that members liked talking about money because it also made them feel they were doing the hard work of a legitimate health organization. This is especially difficult to support because members were invested in distancing themselves from the business model; to acknowledge an interest in conventional legitimacy was to put their alternative identity into question. Yet it's plausible to suggest that members spent so much time on money because it helped them feel good about themselves from both alternative and conventional perspectives. They could believe they were doing the "real work" of a serious organization but in ways that fit their alternative ideals. As we saw in the case of hiring a physician, members valued the conventional. In the next section about fund-raisers as well as in the following chapter, I will show other signs of the value they placed on conventional legitimacy.

FUND-RAISING AS FAILURE

Members' attitudes toward fund-raisers puzzled me at first. Although they found fund-raising events—such as festivals in which practitioners and teachers gave short workshops—valuable and fun, they seemed edgy, then lethargic, when someone suggested that they plan a fund-raising event to make money.

Why did members discuss other ways to make money (in fact, less acceptable ways) with great interest, but have little energy, let alone zeal, when discussing fund-raisers? Fund-raising events, I thought, were morally clean and thus should have reinforced members' collective identity as alternative. What an easy way, it seemed to me, for members to feel good about themselves. Why was it easier for them to use "tainted" means—such as raising fees—to make themselves believe they were living up to alternative ideals?

Fund-raisers were a problem from both the alternative and conventional frames of reference. First, talking about fund-raisers didn't provide members with meaningful opportunities to live out their alternative identity. Second, fund-raisers threatened members' image of themselves as competent organizational actors.

As I expected, members thought of fund-raising as an ethical way to make money. Although raising fees for services was morally questionable for them, fund-raising was not. Members defined fund-raising events as qualitatively different from regular services offered at Renewal. They thought of fund-raisers as voluntary, involving a participant's choice of activity; using a regular health service at Renewal was seen as less voluntary, involving a participant's need. Members, then, regarded participants in fund-raisers as customers or consumers rather than as clients. Fund-raisers were also "clean" because those who put the fund-raiser together usually received little or no pay for their time and effort and charged participants minimal fees.

Eventually I understood that the moral *acceptability* of fund-raisers made them *uninteresting*. Since fund-raisers were clean, participants had trouble fashioning moral dilemmas out of them. Moral dilemmas over money made money interesting. Because fund-raisers were "good" and didn't violate their image as an alternative organization, members found nothing of value to debate about.

Unlike the charged atmosphere in which members discussed other money matters, the air hung heavy in the room during discussions about fund-raisers. Participants spent little time (often no time) figuring out the morally acceptable fee to charge for fund-raisers. Rather, they treated money as neutral, asking largely technical questions: What would the organizing expenses amount to? What would people pay for the event? How much money would Renewal make? Would that amount take care of the immediate money problem? Because fund-raisers were clean, members didn't engage in moral struggles about what to charge. Discussing fund-raisers, then, denied members the opportunity to become impassioned in ways that reinforced their moral identity.

Members became particularly disheartened when someone suggested they put together a fund-raiser as a desperate solution to an immediate financial problem. Why? In the wider culture, fund-raisers are associated with causes rather than business (hence rendering them morally acceptable). But having fund-raisers made it difficult for members to feel that they resembled a legitimate organization. From a conventional, business point of view, fund-raisers are a sign of *failure*. Finding a physician and discussing raises in fees made members feel they were involved in a legitimate organization, but discussing fund-raisers did not. Fund-raising, especially during crises, was the equivalent of bankruptcy.

Why didn't members use the "need" for fund-raisers to reinforce their moral identity? Couldn't they have told themselves that they had to have fund-raisers in order to survive as an alternative organization in a conventional environment? Members' feelings of failure as a business that must "resort to" fund-raisers made it difficult for them to call upon poverty as the moral basis for engaging in money-talk. When they discussed *other* money matters, such as raising fees for services, poverty "beautified"—the moral discussions reinforced their alternative identity while also building up their view of themselves as responsible professionals. In the case of fund-raisers, poverty became a sign of organizational failure and thus brought them down.

Fund-raisers allowed me to see the value members placed on both alternative and conventional legitimacy. If members' only reaction to these discussions had been boredom, this would have supported the hypothesis that members found fund-raisers morally uninteresting and thus valued the alternative perspective *exclusively*. Because members became disheartened and discouraged rather than merely bored, I took this to mean that they lacked a conventional source of legitimacy. In fact, fund-raisers threatened their image of themselves as competent board members. Fund-raisers offered neither interesting moral possibilities nor conventional legitimacy. Their lack of value to members made them valuable to me as I tried to make sense of their reactions. Fund-raisers provided the "deviant case" that supported the more general point that members valued *both* alternative and conventional frames of reference.

WRONG AND RIGHT WAYS TO TALK ABOUT MONEY

Since some board members told me that talking about money was "boring" or "awful," I expected them to apologize when they talked about money at board meetings. Members spent 90 percent of their time at board meetings discussing money or money-related matters, so I expected to hear lots of apologies. Yet when I reread my fieldnotes, I was struck by the *absence* of disclaimers about money-talk at meetings. And those who apologized made others uncomfortable.

Who made disclaimers, how did they make them, and what did these signify to members? Those who had spent little time at Renewal before becoming involved in it tended to talk about money in inappropriate ways. They picked up on the idea that it was unacceptable to *want* to talk about money, but didn't yet understand that *talking* about money also served positive functions for members. In trying to fit in, these newcomers apologized for talking about money. For example, Alicia, who became Director of Renewal for a short time, always began her reports with an apology. At one board meeting she said:

> I want to apologize, but we're not going to have an organization without money. I apologize for being so uptight about it, but without money we won't have an organization.

Alicia suggested that Renewal, by needing money, was indeed poor and hence a true alternative. She seemed to be justifying members' use of a tainted activity (making money) in an alternative organization. Wasn't she doing what other, more experienced members, did?

Apparently not. In these few comments, Alicia turned members off because she suggested that they were failures, both as a legitimate organization and as an alternative. Her statement "We're not going to have an organization without money" insulted those who secretly took pride in Renewal as a serious organization. She implied that being poor is not only organizationally irresponsible but is also the very thing that will stop them from living out their alternative ideals—"without money we won't have an organization." Thus, she had unwittingly made them feel like double failures.

This deviant case highlights why others rarely apologized for talking about money. The plaintive cry that began such discussions— "We really need more money"—differed from Alicia's disclaimer. The lament said to members that they had to talk about money because they were poor, but this poverty resulted from the ideals they embraced, not from disorganization. Presumably they were poor *because* they were doing good.

Alicia paid lip service to the idea that money could corrupt by framing it as a necessary evil. Mostly she treated money as something that responsible organizational members must learn to deal with, an instrumental means to the moral end of maintaining an alternative organization. She followed her introductory statements with proposals for making money (see examples in the next chapter). Doing so kept members from feeling that they were engaged in the kind of talk participants at alternatives were supposed to participate in. Treating money as mundane deprived them of collective experiences that could have reinforced their moral identity. Alicia's words, then, put members' contradictory identity into jeopardy—they were neither truly alternative nor organizationally competent. Board members' *usual* practices buttressed their view of themselves as a legitimate alternative—their moral discussions about money made them feel they were doing serious business within an alternative framework.

Debra, a part-time staff member and board member, volunteered to be on the budget committee. Debra treated Renewal's financial problems as practical matters. She worked hard on the budget but found that others didn't take her suggestions seriously. In an interview after she quit the board, she spoke to me in an exasperated tone:

> Nobody had cared diddly-squat about finances. They felt like it was going to get taken care of somehow, and they didn't worry about anything. And the amazing thing is that they did as well as they did . . . We were spending 13 percent more than we were taking in, so we [the Budget Committee] just cut across the board 13 percent except things we couldn't cut like the rent, utilities. And still people weren't paying much attention to the budget. Then the next time I gave the budget report I felt like I really wasn't getting through to people very well.

She eventually became angry about members' handling of money and other matters:

> Lately, particularly, I get real mad at hippies. When Margaret [an outspoken alternative woman] was on the Board I would just get, uuuh [she shuddered]. I've just got to investigate why I feel this way. Partly I think it's their idea that being businesslike is not humanitarian.

Other members also wanted to be both "businesslike" and "humanitarian." But since members thought that seeking conventional legitimacy contradicted their alternative ideals, they couldn't acknowledge their interest in maintaining a conventional face. The difference, then, between Debra and most other members was this: she didn't see a discrepancy between conventional and alternative ideals. For her, there was no dilemma. Debra's statements, like Alicia's, intimated that members were immature, and thus incapable of running a "real" organization. The term "immature" is apt, for Debra was twenty years older than most members. And, like Alicia, her assumption that money was an instrumental means to a moral end threatened to rob members of the chance to use money to feel like moral actors; at the same time, she made them feel like relative failures at business.

Members approved of Debra's proposals, but they disliked her presentation of them as exclusively technical. It was possible to make budget cuts morally satisfying and organizationally legitimate. When Mike headed the Budget Committee and presented one of his reports, members not only felt satisfied, but were visibly moved. Mike told the board that his committee decided to consult the *I Ching* for answers to Renewal's financial problems. This got members' attention. By consulting the *I Ching*, he implied that money problems are not merely practical matters that require mathematical skills, but cosmic problems that require spiritual guidance. He gave an elaborate description of what the *I Ching* had indicated and how he had interpreted it.

Mike's *conclusion* was the same as Debra's: members needed to make cuts across the board. But the differences between Mike's and Debra's presentations led to dramatically different responses. At the end of his report, Mike gave members a handout with sixty-two ways to "tighten up." He passed around a typed report, with each suggestion numbered from one to sixty-two, thereby giving members an organizational document that they could refer to as a "solution." Thus, he not only made money into a spiritual and thus alternative issue, he also presented his report in a way that legitimated them as a serious organization. Mike legitimated Renewal as an alternative and a "real" organization in a way that kept members from recognizing that they valued the organizational rhetoric of the document—the "spiritualizing" of the document masked the conventional value of it. At the end of the report Frank, the physician referred to earlier, said that of all the board meetings he had attended in his career, none had been as beautiful as that one. Members glowed. The physician had offered his seal of approval—they were indeed a legitimate alternative.

Keeping Things the Same

Members talked about money in ways that maintained their identity as a legitimate alternative. Being in the red proved to them that Renewal was a true alternative. If their resources were greater, members believed, they wouldn't have to resort to such unappealing solutions as hiring a physician or raising fees. The despair and moral negotiation that characterized their money-talk made them feel all the more alternative. At the same time, their serious attitude about money matters built their image of themselves as legit.

Members acknowledged that they were committing a conventional act by raising fees at all. But this was a *safe* confession of conventionality; presumably, they needed to raise fees because they were poor, and their poverty meant that they were indeed living out alternative ideals. Because members' money problems made them feel poor and thus virtuous, talking about their financial crisis at board meetings produced solidarity, especially among central members—the staff and practitioners who served on the board. These feelings of solidarity, however, masked inequalities in the *distribution* of money within the organization. By saying "we are poor," members spoke as if each of them was equally affected by how much money came into Renewal. But only the *staff members'* pay depended on revenues generated by "the organization." Practitioners were paid directly by their clients, and their rent remained low. Thus, the staff and the practitioners were *un*equally poor within Renewal.

The dual nature of the structure made it possible for members to see those who held the most power—the practitioners—as altruistic. Structurally, practitioners were both inside and outside the organization. As private practitioners who collected fees directly from clients and then paid rent to Renewal, they were on the outside. As board members, teachers, and occasional volunteers, they were on the inside. When Renewal "needed more money," members treated practitioners' fees as one possible source. They discussed this as a moral matter with regard to how much a practitioner should charge a client (recall Manny) and how much a practitioner should reasonably pay Renewal for rent and services. In these discussions, then, board members treated the practitioners as another source of "external income" rather than as *part of the organization*. By being financially autonomous in relation to the organization, the practitioners were perceived as benefactors—those who *contributed* to Renewal—rather than as insiders who received the most rewards. From this perspective, it makes sense that the practitioners were seen, and saw themselves, as generous; they "donated" time, energy, and money to Renewal.

The practitioners, especially Ron and Jack, had a privileged position. As the two founding members of Renewal, they were thought of as synonymous with the organization. Yet Ron and Jack had a quasi-outsider position when it came to financial matters, a position they benefited from. Ron and Jack became the patrons who could bestow gifts—status, charisma, time, money—on the organization. In contrast to the "breadwinning" practitioners, the staff members, by being "paid," were seen as draining Renewal's resources.

Ron and Jack's privileged positions were also buttressed by their gender and class. Board members, especially the staff, thought these practitioners could have lucrative, conventional careers, but chose otherwise. Members assumed that Ron and Jack had sacrificed the privileges of professional, middle-class men so that they could do alternative work and act as benefactors for Renewal.

Staff women, on the other hand, had no privileges to sacrifice. As women in womanly jobs, they were expected to do lower-status work without complaining and to feel lucky to receive the "generous gifts" of the male practitioners. The staff women often received no pay for their labor and paid Renewal's bills rather than themselves, but their acts were *not* recognized as sacrifices. The practitioners' incomes were untouched by the poverty of the nonprofit part of the organization, but they had the ability to feed the image of Renewal as poor and thus alternative. Thus, those whose organization-related income depended the *least* on the poor, non-profit part of Renewal had the *most* opportunity to earn others respect by making "sacrifices" to it.

Members' denial of these inequalities was embedded in their apolitical and individualistic notions of equality. They believed that each individual is special and thus deserves equal respect. Hence, they believed that structural or financial arrangements—who got paid what and how—weren't important. Each person, they felt, already *had* equal respect. Believing they had taken care of the problem of inequality by positing that each person is "special," they denied their assumptions about which categories of persons deserve more—or less—at Renewal. Yet such ideas were implicit in their monetary arrangements; staff didn't "need" to be paid much or often, practitioners "needed" to be paid more and shouldn't have to depend on this poor organization to pay them. As in the conventional world, they assumed that the "professionals" of the organization should get more rewards than the staff. By remaining unaware of these assumptions, members could build solidarity around their moral identity.

Because members attributed their poverty to their alternative status, their solutions to their financial problems were always conventional, such as raising fees or hiring a physician. Because they believed they were *already* alternative—indicated by their poverty and their need to discuss making money—the possibility of organizing themselves in more radical ways didn't come up. For example, members didn't discuss whether an egalitarian or communal structure would have worked just as well or better for their "survival problem." Instead, they continued to complain about their financial problems and seek solutions that safely kept alive their identity as a legitimate alternative.

three

CONVENTIONAL SIGNS,
UNCONVENTIONAL COMMITMENTS

RENEWAL WAS SITUATED IN AN OLD HOUSE RATHER THAN an office building; the practitioners saw clients in small bedrooms they had converted to office space. Two practitioners shared each office, and they coordinated their schedules to make sure their clients didn't overlap. Thus, the practitioners didn't have the autonomy that professionals expect to have.

Members occasionally joked about how others perceived them. For example, shortly after Sylvia joined Renewal to practice in the same room as Jack, she raised the following issue at a practitioners meeting:

> "I'd like to talk about putting a chair upstairs instead of the red couch, Jack." Jack said, "Oh, I fixed the couch." Sylvia said, "Well, I'd like to show you the chair. Um, there's a psychiatrist coming to me for supervision, so I suddenly wanted the office to look nice." Jack said, presumably imitating the psychiatrist, "So, *this* is your office? [putting his hand over his mouth and pretending to stifle laughter]. You're a *professional*, right?"

By joking about their broken furniture, members presented themselves as unconcerned about appearing professional. Yet I found that members took many *other* signs of professionalism seriously. Overall, members wanted to think of Renewal as a professional health organization and found ways to convince themselves that it was. They used such *bureaucratic signs* as titles, procedures, rules, committee reports, and minutes of meetings to convince themselves that Renewal was organized rather than chaotic, legitimate rather than flaky.

Didn't a bureaucratic appearance contradict their image of themselves as an alternative organization? Participants in radical organizations in the sixties displayed an *anti*-bureaucratic image; they rejected formal rules and procedures as constraints on creativity and freedom (Rothschild and Whitt 1986). "Structurelessness" (Freeman 1972–73) became an organizational virtue.

Paradoxically, members of Renewal used *conventional* signs to convince themselves that they were committed to their mission as an *alternative*. At times members talked about whether their procedures stifled creativity. These discussions, like their discussions about money, allowed them to believe they were doing alternative "work." Thus, they took a potentially tainted matter—bureaucratic procedures—and used it as a source of moral enhancement and alternative identification.

But members treated many bureaucratic features as untainted rather than as morally problematic. To them, money was inherently evil, but not all bureaucratic signs were bad. By believing that particular bureaucratic features are at worst neutral, members could transform select features into indicators of their commitment to alternative ideals. Hence, it was possible to see a member's adherence to rules as a sign of commitment to the cause rather than as a sign of rigidity.

I treat members' bureaucratic procedures as a "rhetoric of legitimization" (Ball 1970) rather than as objective characteristics of Renewal. For example, whether or not members of an organization *use* the minutes they take of their meetings, *having* minutes can make people feel that what they're doing and where they're doing it are important. In some contexts, the mere presence of bureaucratic signs confers legitimacy on an organization (Meyer and Rowan 1977; DiMaggio and Powell 1983).

Members' belief in the legitimacy of professional-bureaucratic elements was reflected in how they treated each other. But members didn't recognize that they carried their sense of professional-bureaucratic legitimacy into the realm of their own relations. Their individualistic ideology—the idea that each person is unique, special, and equal—led them to believe that they treated everyone the same, regardless of title.

FORMING A PROFESSIONAL-BUREAUCRATIC IMAGE

Reporting to the Board

The board was the chief operating body of Renewal and handled all matters, large and small. Even the simplest task could not be done without board approval, and participants had to report back to the board when they made small changes in their original plans. There were many committees at Renewal, and all committee chairs had to report to the board at each meeting, even when they had nothing to report. Chairs gave lengthy presentations over small events.

Committee reports and other procedures had a legitimating function for members. The barrage of reports made members feel that they were participating in an organization that had a lot going on. Attending to the details of organization meant that they were serious professionals. That having committees was a sign of legitimacy was captured in the remarks of Cal, a practitioner–board member, at a board meeting:

> "I'd like to propose that we make a booklet on the committees, who's who on them, so we know who needs help. I'm thinking of the Town Church. I was there this morning and they had that kind of booklet, explaining their structure and what the committees do. A page on each. I was *impressed*." Others nodded in agreement.

Those with the fewest roles at Renewal—board members who were neither practitioners nor staff members—questioned the board's control and the preponderance of bureaucratic procedures. For example, Willie, a new board member, said they should spend less time on committee reports and they could do this if they limited the discussion to chairs who actually had something to say. The core members replied with comments such as "It's important to have everyone check in," and "It's good to know what's going on."

Those who were doing intermittent projects for Renewal also objected to the board's degree of control, finding it an impediment to their work. For example, when Lenny, a non-board member and marginal practitioner (he worked only two hours a week at Renewal), volunteered to work on setting up a program for people who wanted to learn low-level healing skills, he came to the board meeting and said:

> "I don't want to come back every time I have a handout. It seems to me that's what committees are for. So I want to know where I fit in." Ron said, "Well, we could make it a staff level committee and you could communicate with us through Alicia [the Director]" . . . Mike, a community board member, said, "Wait a minute. Who's staff anyway? Do we have more than two or three staff, or any?" Ron said, "Yes. Two or three." Mike said, "But *all* committees are board level because board members are always on them, right?" No one responded to Mike's comments and they went on to discuss Lenny's work with enthusiasm.

Mike's comment met with silence because it put the "complexity" of the organization into question. If members admitted that there was much overlap in their committees, then they'd have trouble believing that Renewal was big enough to house multiple committees with a variety of people with different skills. If committees had many of the same members on them, then their long list of committees created a false image of organizational complexity. Significantly, examining their committees would have made it apparent that their central committees were top-heavy with practitioner–board members.

Having members report to the board for the smallest of matters gave board members a lot of control over Renewal business. But not everyone *wanted* this much control, as we saw in the comments of those who lacked multiple roles at Renewal (I will return to a discussion of these community board members later in this chapter). Board members with the most power understandably wanted to know what everyone was doing in order to maintain control.

What about staff–board members? Carla and Jane, two staff members who were on the board, felt (for a time) that they had two important functions—working for Renewal and being board members. But in practice this meant that they brought reports of their staff work to other board members, who then approved or disapproved of what they did or planned to do. At the same time, they had less influence over other board matters, because the practitioner–board members were perceived as being more "in the know."

Carla and Jane joined practitioners in defending the board's control over daily matters and the use of various bureaucratic procedures. Why? Identifying with the practitioners—those with the most power—and less so with community board members—those least invested in the organization—made them feel like powerful members of Renewal. The bureaucratic procedures and the board's control over organizational matters enhanced the status of the board. As those with the least power, staff members needed the legitimacy of the board. That legitimacy helped them feel they were part of a powerful board that closely oversaw the operations of a complex organization. But these feelings of equality also masked Ron and Jack's greater power.

Sacred Minutes

Members rotated the task of taking the minutes at board meetings and handing out copies of them to board members at the start of each meeting. What did members do with the minutes? Members skimmed rather than read the minutes, and often thanked the person who had written them. "Accepting the minutes" was an agenda item, and except for one set, members approved them. Over time I noticed that members gave the most praise to those who had put together the most official-looking minutes. Minutes that had a bureaucratic look—lengthy, well-typed, with lots of headings, subheadings, and underlinings—received more thank-yous and positive comments than those that had a few typos and chatty remarks.

Members rarely referred back to the minutes, even when they couldn't remember what decisions they had reached at a previous meeting. Yet the minutes, as an authority prop, had a lot of significance. This only became clear to me when someone wrote what I referred to in my field notes as "alternative minutes." Margaret, who had just joined the board, took the minutes for her first—

and last—time. She did not type the minutes (everyone else did) but made copies of her handwritten notes. Her notes omitted the usual list of resolutions at the top of page one. Instead, she began with the first issue and had notes on what members talked about. Then she went on to the next issue. Margaret's minutes were different not only for what she left out but also for what she added. She interwove drawings with her words, including one of a nude woman.

Margaret didn't attend the next meeting, although she brought her minutes to Renewal earlier in the day. Someone handed them out. As members looked through the minutes, some of them started to fidget. A few had angry looks on their faces.

> Ron spoke with controlled anger: "I object to how Margaret took the minutes. She didn't follow the format. This is really unclear." Barry, a community board member, seemed amused by others' angry responses. He said, smiling, "Ron, it takes time to draw pictures!" Debra, who rented a room to Margaret, said "I'll cut off her electricity!" Debra was joking, but her disapproval of the minutes was clear. Other core board members made snide comments about the minutes. They spent about twenty minutes rewriting them, line by line. I was struck by the effort they put into these revisions, since I had never seen anyone use the minutes.

Margaret, in this instance as in several others, violated norms. A volunteer and occasional staff member, she was more outspoken than other staff women and sometimes challenged the practitioners' motives. She differed from core members in one important way—she lacked a secret longing for conventional legitimacy or a professional face. In my interview with her after she quit the board, she sarcastically referred to core members' discussions about rules and procedures as "playing grown-up."

Margaret's minutes documented the feel of the meeting, and her artwork offered her personal stamp. But only *im*personal minutes can evoke objectivity and authority. Since others considered Margaret the most alternative person they knew, why didn't they use her minutes to reinforce their image of themselves as unconventional? Margaret's alternative displays, including her minutes, made members nervous because they didn't *also* give members the opportunity to believe they were doing real organizational work. Yet, because members wouldn't openly express their interest in appearing legitimate, they didn't chastise Margaret for failing to live up to conventional norms. Rather, they defined her rule breaking as a sign of lack of commitment to the *alternative* mission. They said her minutes indicated a lack of care for Renewal and thus also for the cause (holistic health). Their interpretation kept them from seeing that Margaret's minutes bothered them because they robbed members of one sign of organizational legitimacy.

Barry, a community board member, questioned the value of formal procedures and documents and valued alternative renditions of them. Like Mike and Lenny in the case of committee reports, Barry questioned procedures that seemed to have no practical purpose.

Why did they react differently from core members? These three men had other sources of conventional legitimacy: day jobs outside Renewal. They saw their participation at Renewal as volunteer work that made them feel they hadn't left the sixties behind. Barry, who reacted strongly against formal procedures and had the most appreciation for Margaret, was a physician. Being on the board of Renewal allowed him to believe he hadn't sold out.

Core members also found ways to reinforce their alternative identity. But they were also trying to legitimate themselves as professional and, unlike community board members, depended solely on Renewal for that sense of legitimacy. Committee reports and official-looking minutes served as double legitimators for core members. But community board members needed Renewal to reinforce only their *alternative* identity. Participating only intermittently, they needed to believe that Renewal was alternative enough to give them a strong dose of difference that could last for the two weeks between each board meeting. For their purposes, "anti-minutes" worked better than those that looked bureaucratic. If Renewal mirrored conventional organizations, why participate? They would only have been reinforcing their already secure conventional identity.

The section of the minutes that members read rather than skimmed was the list of people who had attended the previous meeting. Members thought of attendance at board meetings as a serious matter that indicated commitment to Renewal and thus to holistic health. Members had a rule that anyone who missed more than three meetings in a row should be dismissed from the board. This didn't mean that members immediately dismissed the person. But they noted anyone who broke the rule and discussed at length whether that person should be allowed to continue. In the two instances in which this occurred, members decided to let the individuals stay on the board, but only after much discussion about whether their reasons for having missed meetings were valid.

Occasionally, the person who took the minutes left out someone who had been present. If the person whose name had been omitted attended the next meeting, he or she always corrected it. For example, on one occasion Karen noted that her name was absent. She asked, "Did this happen because I came in late?" Jane, on another occasion, said, "I've been left off the minutes. I was here. This is the second time this has happened." Members didn't refer to the minutes to check if someone had missed a few meetings; rather, they asked each other about it. Still, members wanted *official* recognition.

Such recognition seemed especially important to staff members, those who identified strongly with the organization but had the least power within it. Although others' names were occasionally omitted, only Jane, Carla, and Karen (a novice practitioner who had been Ron's apprentice) became distraught when this happened. For them, board membership enhanced their lower position in the organization. Having their names omitted from the minutes reflected the invisibility of the positions they occupied. Understandably, they wanted to be seen and acknowledged.

Outsiders as Legitimators

Members occasionally delegated some organizational tasks to outsiders or people who had weak connections to Renewal. At one point, they hired an "official" fund-raiser. At another point, they created a committee, composed mostly of those who had minimal participation in Renewal, to figure out how to improve Renewal organizationally and financially. A graduate student pursuing an MBA studied Renewal for a term paper. And I became something of a sociologist-in-residence.

Having consultants (my word), especially those with conventional credentials, legitimated them as a serious organization. But how did members have consultants without recognizing that they valued the legitimacy these consultants brought to Renewal? Members defined their "need" for help from outsiders as indicative of their alternative status. Having *some* degree of organizational ineptness reinforced their image of themselves as unconventional.

Members' decision to find consultants, or accept the ones who came to their door, allowed them to feel they were acting responsibly as board members and as alternative actors. Their ineptness meant they had loftier, alternative matters to deal with; the solution, to get help from others, meant that they were willing to act responsibly. In addition, members felt virtuous about having outsiders around because it meant that they were willing to let others monitor them. Recall Carla's words when I talked to her about the possibility of studying Renewal; she wanted my "objective" view. That word had the weight of conventional legitimacy as well as the unspoken "even if it hurts." Members, then, used outsiders who had some conventional legitimacy (in my case, a university faculty member) to increase their sense of legitimacy while reinforcing their collective image as those who sacrificed for the alternative cause.

What did outsiders do and how did members react to them? Katherine Mason, an MBA student, studied Renewal for a class. She interviewed key members of Renewal, examined budgets, and wrote a report. She worked with the newly created Personnel Committee. Katherine and the committee were supposed to write a proposal for improving the financial state of the organization. The committee had no members from the core group in Renewal; board members said they'd get an "objective view" by having relative outsiders do the work. Of the five people on the committee, three were affiliated with Renewal but were neither board members, staff members, nor longtime practitioners. One was a new practitioner and the other was a former board member.

Katherine and three members of the committee gave their report at a board meeting. They said the board was too involved in the daily running of Renewal and should be concerned only with long-term policy issues. They suggested Renewal hire an Executive Director to replace the current Coordinator (Carla) and Business Manager (Jane). As the discussion continued, it became clear that

Carla had told the committee she was planning to leave her position. But Jane had no interest in leaving. Katherine said to Jane, "I was told that you didn't want to be Business Manager." Jane's expression was pained as she said, "That's news to me. I didn't know I felt that way."

Members talked about whether the committee had put "profits before people." Jack said, "My concern is with people's personal feelings, even though it [the committee's suggestion] could be financially good for Renewal." Jane added, "I'd like to know if the Personnel Committee thought about the people and not just the positions." Arthur, a member of the committee, said, "You mean if it displaces someone's job? We thought about that a lot. Without Renewal there won't be any jobs *or* people. So Renewal has to come first." Jane said plaintively, "I don't understand what you're saying. I'd like to think that if I left Renewal now, it would be in trouble."

Some board members raised other issues. Margaret said, "There was this hush-hush about the committee, and there seems to be a speedy aggression here. I get nervous when there's secrecy. It seems like it was four people [actually, five] working exclusively."

The Personnel Committee violated norms about how meetings were run. Typically, meetings were fairly free-flowing. In theory, participants could speak as much and as often as they wished. At times, meetings ran on until midnight. Given the significance of the topic—reorganizing Renewal—members felt there was all the more reason to let people have their say. But Katherine started the meeting with a rule: "So this won't go on all night, we've decided that each person should say what you want to say in three minutes. If you can, write it down, 'cause that'll make it clearer. You can ask as many questions as you want, but comments should be limited to three minutes." Although members didn't complain immediately, some angry comments surfaced later in the meeting. Bob said angrily, "This is as much my board meeting as any other fuckin' board meeting, and I resent the Personnel Committee telling me how to discuss *this* board meeting." Jack added, "I don't like the fact that the Personnel Committee gets to talk all they want, and we get three minutes."

The instrumental attitude of members of the Personnel Committee bothered members more than their specific recommendations. For example, Joanne, the Chair of the committee, stated,

"For a business to operate—and you are a business—you need a central person, with authority. Without money, you're wasting your time." Ron coughed loudly and gave Joanne a dirty look. Others bristled. Like Alicia's comments about money (in the previous chapter), Joanne's remarks threatened them from both alternative and conventional standpoints. Her blunt remarks turned money into an instrumental, and thus a nonmoral, issue. And she suggested that they were acting irresponsibly as a board.

Members voted to hold a retreat a few weeks later to deal with people's feelings about what had transpired. At that time, the committee members justified their proposals by saying that they had taken their task—to make a more efficient organization—seriously. They blamed the outsider—the MBA student—for the cold tone of the meeting and for setting up the three-minute limit. Katherine didn't attend the retreat.

Resolving the crisis created anxiety and took up a lot of time and energy. Members talked about this incident for a couple of months, during and outside their meetings. But as I suggested (in the previous chapter) in the case of Manny's proposed fee hike, the extended angst wasn't necessarily a burden. Through their passionate discussion about values—people versus profits—members felt engaged in an authentic alternative. In addition, having a clash with outsiders created solidarity among members and reinforced their image of themselves as different.

Similar to the crisis over Manny, the actions of the Personnel Committee gave members the experience of moral renewal. By *disagreeing* with their consultants, members hid their interest in having some conventional legitimacy. They could tell themselves that they were unmistakably different from those "on the outside." The mere presence of consultants generated feelings of legitimacy among members; consultants only had to come around intermittently to boost members' esteem. And turning their consultants' attitude and recommendations into moral issues further reinforced members' image as alternative.

Once things settled down, the board agreed to hire a Director (as the committee had recommended). Jane stayed on as Business Manager. The Director was put in charge of the staff, but wasn't allowed to become a member of the board. Keeping the Director off the board maintained control of Renewal by the board, which largely meant control by Jack and Ron. But Ron and Jack had increased, rather than decreased, others' trust in them over this event. Jack argued against the three-minute limit and indirectly supported Jane, the staff member who almost lost her job, when he said: "My concern is with people's personal feelings, even though it could be financially good for Renewal." Ron stayed on core members' good side when he reacted against Joanne's push to take a more businesslike approach to Renewal. Overall, then, things remained the same.

Members' acceptance of conventional legitimacy can also be seen in their choice of a Director. The committee decided on Alicia, someone few people knew. Committee members emphasized that Alicia had two postgraduate degrees and had administered a large grant. The other main candidate was Josh, a "friend" of Renewal who had taught classes there and was well liked by several board members. Not hiring Josh upset a few members:

> "I want to feel her [Alicia's] personhood. I want to feel that somehow she'll be better than Josh." Karen said, "That was a real problem in doing this. We all like Josh, and it was very difficult. And I don't see how you can expect to love a new person who walks in the room the way you love Josh, who we all know. Give it time."

The problem in hiring Alicia, it seemed, lay mostly in how committee members presented their choice. They only talked about her credentials. Once the issue of her "personhood" was raised, committee members talked in excited tones about her. They mentioned that she sews her own clothes and is a great cook. Those who were disappointed that Josh wouldn't be joining them seemed to relax. (I will return later to these gendered comments about Alicia.)

Rosemary, also unknown to most members, asked if she could work for the organization as a fund-raiser. She proposed that she'd receive a percentage of whatever funds she raised for Renewal. If she failed to bring in money, Renewal wouldn't owe her anything. A few members confided to me that they thought Rosemary wasn't quite their kind of person. They found her too well groomed, too fancy, and overly enthusiastic. Why did they accept Rosemary's request? Recall that members felt they could be businesslike about fund-raising, because they thought of it as morally unproblematic. By having an *official* fund-raiser they could also diminish their sense of failure as a business that needed to do fundraising.

Rosemary and Alicia came up with the idea of creating an advisory board for Renewal. They wanted to find "prominent people in the community" to agree to be on the board and then list their names in Renewal's newsletter and membership bulletin. Alicia presented the idea to the board. She said, straightforwardly, that advisory board members wouldn't do much of anything; they'd meet once a year to discuss Renewal's policies. She made it clear that the purpose of the advisory board was to legitimate Renewal to various segments of the community. She hoped that listing the names on the masthead would generate more clients, memberships, and donations.

As Alicia talked about this idea, I became nervous for her. She seemed unaware of the criticisms that surely would follow. Hadn't she learned to present instrumental ideas in moral terms? Although members liked the idea of having an advisory board, they criticized Alicia for saying that the board would exist only to enhance their image. They also said they should be selective about who'd be on the board. Rosemary recommended a physician she planned to talk to. Sam said, "I know that doctor,and I think he's fine. But I don't think we should get just *anybody* who might do it. It should be an *honor*." Others nodded.

At the next board meeting, they came back to this issue. Alicia mentioned two potential candidates. Ron said, "It's hard to judge these names in isolation. Why don't we get, say, twenty names and select a few. Then we can compare. It'll take longer, but . . ." Alicia replied, "Well, most will probably refuse. We're doing this a lot for status, and these people won't have much to do with Renewal." Members froze. Several said they were *not* doing this for status. Jack suggested they each bring in names the next time.

At that meeting, members went over a long list of names. Most of the people on the list had conventional occupations that they practiced in some less-than-conventional ways. For example, they approved a dentist who used nonmercury fillings. A few psychotherapists were accepted. Another was the owner of a popular vegetarian restaurant. A few professors in health-related fields were nominated, as was a pediatrician they referred to as "a good guy."

By turning the advisory board into a moral issue, members reinstated themselves as alternative actors, yet still legitimated themselves through conventional means. Because they scrutinized those who were nominated for the board rather than accepting any prominent people who might agree to serve, members believed they were *un*concerned with legitimacy. But as members talked, it became clear that the advisory board would meet only a few times a year. In addition, the kinds of people members approved—those with conventional titles—differed little from the list generated by Alicia and Rosemary. Although members rejected Alicia and Rosemary's attitude, they came up with a similar product. But the *process* members engaged in allowed them to create a legitimating board without having to acknowledge that they cared about having one. They had, once again, managed to buttress their moral identity through conventional resources.

Practitioners as Professionals

Practitioners met every other week. At these meetings, they reinforced their collective image as legitimate healers who were building a serious health organization.

The practitioners had an extensive application procedure that itself legitimated their seriousness. Each applicant filled out a long application, submitted three letters of reference, went through a review by the practitioners, and gave a presentation of his or her service to at least one practitioner (usually more than one attended). Sylvia, who initially worried that the practitioners wouldn't find her particular therapy unconventional enough, said at a meeting that she "was impressed with the application procedures." She hadn't worked anywhere where she had been screened so thoroughly. She didn't say directly that she expected an alternative health center to have looser standards than a conventional health organization, but her tone gave her away. She looked embarrassed as others teased her for being surprised by their conscientiousness.

The practitioners shared small rooms and had no space in the building to add more therapists. Yet they spent hours, in and out of meetings, going over applications from those who showed an interest in practicing at Renewal. In one case, members were so excited about an applicant that they agreed to ask her to give a demonstration of her practice (the second stage of their application procedure). That decision jolted one of the practitioners out of the collective reverie: "We can't do this! We have no room to hire her, so it's not fair to put her through the next stage." Everyone agreed.

But the practitioners continued to look over applications. A relatively new practitioner who worked at Renewal only two hours a week suggested that they stop going over applications until a room opened up. After they had spent about an hour going over a particular application,

> Harry said, "I thought we weren't going to go through this until we get more space. I don't see the point in doing this every time." Jack said, "I think it's important to do this. We're not being inundated with applications; I think it's important to know what kinds of services we want." The others nodded.

Harry didn't recognize that their discussions served a legitimating function. Through their talk, the practitioners acted like "real professionals," an exclusive group that decided who was worthy of membership in "their" organization. Discussing the applications also legitimated the practitioners' efforts by helping them believe that they would expand in the future. Believing they would build a bigger and better health center in the future reinforced the seriousness of their intentions in the present.

The practitioners spent a lot of time discussing whether an applicant's therapy had merit. This was a tricky matter; they thought of themselves as offering a home for therapies considered flaky by the medical establishment, yet they wanted to accept only "serious" therapies:

> Karen had written a letter of reference for Malcolm. She said, "I took his course [at Renewal] and I know him as a friend. The thing about the service is that the effects are very subtle, and most people aren't aware enough of themselves to notice the effects. [She paused.] I'm ashamed to bring it up, but I think a lot of people out there will think it's flaky. But then again, if we're something new and we aren't on the edge, who will be?"

Like those who have achieved the honorific title of professional (Becker 1970), members decided who was worthy of being a practitioner and who was a quack. But they wanted to judge others without feeling they were being exclusionary. For members, being elitist was morally unacceptable. By making a moral issue out of screening applicants, members convinced themselves that they worried about exclusivity and hence were living out alternative ideals. They interpreted their *anxiety* about whether their tastes in therapy had become too conventional as a sign that they had not "sold out."

In addition, since some of the practitioners knew the applicants in other contexts, usually as friends, they felt uncomfortable about rejecting them. This issue can come up in any organization, conventional or alternative. But at Renewal, saying that someone was a good friend meant that he or she was a good person, and personhood was an important criterion for being a healer. For example, after a lengthy discussion about one applicant, Jack said, "I don't hear any good reason to accept her except for personal liking." Ron said, "And that's a good reason." Jack paused, looked sheepish, and said softly, "You're right." They continued to talk about the applicant. Finally, they decided that her therapy wasn't the best one for Renewal "right now."

Karen reacted against the language of "accepting" or "rejecting" an applicant. This wording made it difficult to conceal that they were making judgments about inclusion and exclusion. During one meeting, Jack said, "All those in favor of accepting Maggie?" No hands were raised. He then said, "All those in favor of rejecting her?" Karen said, "Could you word that differently? I don't like the word 'rejection.'" Jack replied, "We're just rejecting her for now. All right. All those in favor of not accepting her now?" They all raised their hands.

Practitioners' discussions made members feel that they were acting like real professionals but doing so in ways that reinforced their alternative identity. They believed they had a protective role for Renewal and for clients—to keep those who had flaky practices away from them. When someone (usually Karen), showed concern about excluding a new, important therapy that *appeared* flaky, talking about it made them feel they were taking alternative matters seriously. As in the case of other organizational procedures, their lengthy discussions lent them professional *and* alternative legitimacy.

At their meetings, the practitioners talked openly about seeing themselves as the central players at Renewal. Occasionally, they referred to themselves as "the professionals." This usually came up when members accused each other of acting *unlike* professionals. They didn't use the term unprofessional to question their particular services, but to make others feel bad for coming late to meetings. Whether they used the word professional or not, members made it quite clear to each other that they had a pivotal role in the organization:

> Jack said, "I feel the need to talk about these meetings, like how important they are to us, how often we should have them. Manny scheduled a client, I could have done that. Ron's got a cold, and Karen's out getting a soda right now. I'm concerned that our attendance is getting smaller." Sarah said, "I think they're very important. If not, I wouldn't drive thirty-four miles to get here. It's all I'm in town for. My time is very valuable to me; time is the most valuable resource we have. So it's very important." Cal said, "I think these meetings are very valuable. We're most directly responsible for Renewal, and this is one way to get to know what's going on. I find it's really helpful to throw things out here and discuss them." The others nodded.

The practitioners saw themselves not only as caring the most about holistic health but also as having made the greatest sacrifices for the cause and for Renewal. Since they saw themselves as having *given things up* for Renewal, they failed to see what they *gained* from their position. Lacking awareness of their privileges, they didn't recognize themselves as the elite who got to make decisions that others didn't, nor as the group that received the most pay and had the most influence over others.

It's not surprising that those who have privileges see their position as natural rather than as constructed. But how did other members of Renewal see the practitioners? According to members' ideology, titles and positions are superficial and say nothing about the essential worth of a person. Labels such as "Chair of the Board," "practitioner," and "staff member" are merely that—labels that stand for particular tasks without carrying judgment about the *value* of the position. Yet, to someone looking in, these positions brought incumbents blatantly unequal privileges—materially, symbolically, and emotionally.

Members denied differences in *authority* among positions, but in an unspoken way they agreed that the positions of practitioner, Chair of the Board, and Program Committee Chair had more responsibility and carried more weight. And they viewed those who took on more responsibility as those who had the greatest commitment to holistic health. Hence, having multiple roles at Renewal—board member, practitioner, teacher—meant that one was highly committed to the cause. Ron and Jack each played these three roles.

But not all multiple involvements were equal. Members' perceptions of a person's degree of organizational responsibility depended on *which* positions one held. For example, staff members who were also board members and volunteers weren't seen as having a lot of responsibility. These women ran the nonprofit part of Renewal, helped out the practitioners, and kept Renewal alive by paying utilities and rent rather than themselves. Even those who held the title "Director" (first Alicia, and later, Jane) didn't get the same respect. Members didn't treat the staff's responsibilities as valuable.

At Renewal, members thought of the practitioners as having spent time, money, and energy to become therapists and to build their practices. They also saw them as having *sacrificed* the promise of greater salaries and conventional authority in order to practice alternative medicine and work in an unconventional organization. That these practitioners were willing to take on positions of responsibility in an alternative organization buttressed their authority. By having privileges to give up, they became eligible for others' respect. The staff women, on the other hand, had nothing to sacrifice that could bring them honor in the organization.

Although some community board members hinted that the practitioners had too much power on the board, these same members also came to think of the practitioners as those who did the most for Renewal. Initially, they thought the practitioners on the board might have a conflict of interest, especially because the board decided such matters as how much rent the practitioners should pay. Over time, they came to see the practitioners' multiple involvements as indicating their loyalty to the organization. Why did this change of heart happen? The community board members' main contact with Renewal was at board meetings. There, the practitioners were the most vocal, certainly more than the core staff members who sat on the board. As the community board members began to feel guilty about their own lack of involvement, their trust in and respect for the practitioners increased. For example, months after he joined the board, Mike said to me:

> This [multiple involvements] is a problem. Usually, boards are people without vested interests in the organization. All these overlapping interests can make for trouble. But at the same time it makes sense that the people most involved should be making decisions. I feel guilty that I don't do more around Renewal.

By believing that the practitioners had the most responsibility and had made the most sacrifices, members maintained the practitioners' basis of privilege. Participants were *grateful* that practitioners like Jack and Ron were willing to remain involved in Renewal. They failed to recognize that Ron and Jack had authority precisely because members thought they had given it up.

THE LIMITS OF FORMAL ORGANIZATION

We have seen that members used bureaucratic features to enhance their dual image without having to recognize the value they placed on conventionality. Here I'll examine incidents in which members *challenged* particular procedures. Specifically, I'll examine what happened when Jack, the person with the most power in the organization, tried to get members to adopt Robert's Rules of Order.

At one board meeting, Jack asked board members to leave notes with him about any changes they'd like to see in the running of the board meetings. About a month later, he told the board that he had used Robert's Rules of Order to come up with a handout (reproduced below) that described how he thought their future meetings should be run. To a group that prided itself on process, the handout came as a surprise. I include it here to show the degree of detail, the formality of the document, and the clamp it put on discussion.

GUIDELINES FOR MEETINGS
Board of Directors
Renewal

The purpose of these guidelines is to allow the Board to more effectively fulfill its function while protecting the needs and liberties of individuals. These "rules" come from the past practice of Renewal, suggestions from Board members, and *Robert's Rules of Order*.

AGENDA
The regular order of business shall be:

Meeting called to order by presiding officer. (May be opened with circle, etc.)
Meetings begin at 7:30.
Reading of minutes (with changes and approval)
Board committee reports
Director's report and staff committee reports
Unfinished business, itemized
New business, itemized
Announcements, as convenient
Recesses, if appropriate (e.g., during unusually long meetings)
Adjournment by presiding officer (usually by 10 p.m.)

Note: To facilitate efficiency and insure inclusion of new business on the agenda, all agenda items should be given to the chairperson or secretary, in written form if possible, before 7:30 p.m. on the night of a board meeting.

MOTIONS—proposals that require Renewal action, commitment, or consideration of any subject.

In order to make a motion, a *member* of the Board must *obtain the floor* (as recognized by chairperson). (All *main motions* should be presented *in writing* to the chair or secretary before they are made.)

1) the member then states, as *clearly and simply* as possible, the content of the motion. In order for the motion to be open to *debate* and *vote*,

2) another member must second the motion. Suggestions for alterations (*not debate*) can be made to the member who proposed the motion. This member can modify, or withdraw the motion anytime before the chair states the motion to the Board.

3) The Chair then states the motion. The question is now before the Board for debate.

A. The member whose motion is under consideration is recognized as having the floor first during discussions (in most circumstances). Other members may obtain recognition for the floor by the chairperson.

B. No member who has once had the floor is again entitled to it while the same question is before the Board, if the floor is claimed by one who has not spoken to that question.

C. As the interests of Renewal are best served by alternating points of view on a question, the chair should give preference to a speaker whose point of view opposed the preceding speaker (while maintaining above principles A and B).

D. No member shall speak more than twice to the same question, nor for more than five minutes at one time, without permission of the Board (2/3 vote, without debate).

DEBATE

After a motion is made and seconded it is stated by the chairperson. It is then open to debate following the guidelines under MOTIONS.

Undebatable Questions (Those starred once (*) require a majority vote; those starred twice (**) can be decided or called by the chair if there is no objection or appeal; those starred three times (***) must have 2/3 in favor to pass.)

To fix the time to adjourn or to adjourn**
Orders of the day (and priority of business)**
Appeals (and questions of order)**
Objection to consideration of a question***
Lay on the table (postpone until voted to take from table)*
Previous question (the present question - decision to vote)***
To reconsider (the vote of a previous question)*
Withdrawing a motion**
Extending time limits***
Suspending the rules***
Limiting or closing debate***
Postpone to a certain time (limited debate)*

In debate, it is very advisable that members confine discussion to the questions before the Board, and not to personalities. It is appropriate to respond to the nature or consequences of a motion as strongly as one thinks/feels, but not to attack or condemn individuals.

VOTE

When all members have had the opportunity to speak (on debatable questions), the chair will ask the

Board if they are ready for the question. If there are no objections and no superseding motions, a vote of the affirmative and negative will be taken. For record keeping, only the yes and no votes will be recorded unless a member requests her/his name be entered into the minutes with the vote.

For most motions, a simple majority of a quorum is needed. A quorum is one member more than half.

Much discussion and debate followed. Board members agreed that their meetings could be better organized, but felt that Robert's Rules were too rigid and stifling. Members reacted strongly against item D, that "no member shall speak more than twice to the same question, nor for more than five minutes at one time, without permission of the Board (2/3 vote, without debate)."

Vicky said, "I don't like the idea of having limits on the time it takes to present an idea. What's so special about a five-minute limit? And this business about not being able to speak more than twice on the same issue." Margaret said, "I'd like some understanding of why you chose Robert's Rules? Aren't there any other models?"

Members said that some of the rules violated the value they placed on process. Jack wanted members to write down any agenda items before the meeting started and also to write down rather than state their motions during the meetings. These rules went against their notion that debate or discussion is a process that cannot be determined in advance. Members felt that this would preempt spontaneity and creativity. Predictably, Margaret's reaction was the strongest and the most negative: "We assume that when a sentence is out there, it's the 'real thing,' otherwise it's less. The rules do nothing to help us work synergistically. I think these rules represent polarity and will create more of it." Margaret's statement hinted at the legitimating function of formal rules by pointing out that in this society, written documents have more authority than oral statements.

Alicia, the new Director, tried to make the rules seem less rule-like. She said, "I think this is good [looking at Jack's handout]. Even with these rules I don't think it'll stifle us—not *this* group!" Alicia tried to reinforce their identity as an alternative by suggesting that members were too unconventional to live up to the rules, even if they accepted them "on paper." The debate became heated.

Jack said, "It's been my most challenging task as Chairperson so far trying to come up with these guidelines. These are the rules the legislative bodies in this country use." Ron, who had been quite favorable towards the rules until that point said sarcastically, "Oh, great. That makes me sick." Lisa sounded uncharacteristically sarcastic when she said, "Yes, let's do it because it's the American way." Jack said in a serious tone, "This is the *I Ching* of the legislative bodies." Karen came to Jack's defense and said, "Just because there's corruption in the government doesn't mean the rules of legislation are all wrong." Margaret jumped in, "What do you do if someone has a fit? Do you have cops? Do we put them in the next room? In the 'fit room'?" Jack said angrily to Margaret, "Margaret, I wish you'd turn your authoritarianism to *our* side."

Jack's direct hit at Margaret redeemed him to the group. His words echoed what others told me privately, that Margaret was too pushy. Some found her a contradiction. They thought that because she had far-out ideas she should have been tolerant, rather than critical, of different points of view.

Unlike Margaret, other core members wanted to believe that their ordered minutes and committee reports meant something. Still, they were in a bind because they felt that Jack's recommendations went too far. Lisa said:

> I know we have a problem here. On the one hand we want to be an alternative organization and deal with people's feelings. But then there's the practical, mundane things we have to deal with that have to get done. I think we should try Robert's Rules for a couple of weeks even though I feel a bit queasy about it. I think we might also try to come up with a more unique way of making rules and not just stick to Robert's Rules.

Lisa intimated that they needed to act in conventional ways at times in order to deal with "practical, mundane things." As in the case of money, this statement suggested that they had to find some way (though not necessarily Robert's Rules) to get things done. Lisa sounded sad as she talked. Soon others, too, moved the issue from Jack's "going too far" to a lament over how difficult it was to be a "true" alternative.

Members felt good about their discussion of Robert's Rules. Their passionate debate about what they perceived as a moral matter made them feel they were participating in a true alternative. By treating rules as morally problematic, they felt they were resisting conformity. They had limits. Members agreed to change rule D (to allow members more than five minutes discussion and more than one turn to talk). This satisfied everyone but Margaret. By the next meeting, Jack said he forgot to bring Robert's Rules to the meeting and suggested they forget them for that day. He, and others, dropped any references to Robert's Rules after that. As far as I could tell, the meetings were unchanged.

How did this event affect Jack's position? Did he lose credibility as their unacknowledged leader? Jack was the person who best fit their contradictory ideals and in that sense personified Renewal. He was one of the two remaining founding members of Renewal and the best-known healer. Hence, members associated him with the "mission." He also offered conventional legitimacy through his degrees, his work experience, and his organizational skills. Others' belief in Jack's competence in his multiple roles minimized their insecurities about *both* the legitimacy of Renewal and the board's commitment to an alternative orientation.

Jack's "transgression" reinforced his image as organized— only someone who was well organized could go overboard. Although some lost credibility for putting efficiency first (recall Alicia and Rosemary), Jack could retain his authoritative position because people already thought of him as committed to holistic healing. (Others assumed that staff members couldn't be similarly committed because they hadn't given up high-status jobs and salaries to work at Renewal.) Thus, members defined Jack's labors as signs of organizational commitment. They thanked him for the time he took to put together the handout and told him that they knew he had good intentions. For those who had the lingering sense that Jack had too much power, fighting him on the issue of Robert's Rules allowed them to feel Jack didn't run things, that they disagreed with him when they saw fit.

Members occasionally teased Jack about being over-organized. Instead of seeing him as rigid and unworthy of his esteemed status in the organization, members turned his style into a quirk of personality. Their interpretation made Jack's style endearing because it meant that he was, like them, a little bit crazy, and thus human. At Renewal, those who had authority couldn't maintain others' trust without keeping up what Bennett Berger (1981) calls their "human credentials." For example, at a practitioner meeting Jack said:

> "I'd like to discuss soundproofing. I find it noisy, like when someone slams the bathroom door. There's a crack under the door and foam could be put there to make it better. When I'm with a client and that person is nervous and there needs to be quiet to go into a trance, it's really bad when there are these noises. You can hear someone urinating in the bathroom or hear them slam the door. I think we'll all benefit from doing something about that." Manny said, "I haven't noticed that." Karen said, "Me neither. Gee, I think you're going too far with this. I mean, *really.*" Manny said, smiling, "I think we need a party where we can piss and make noise." Everyone but Jack and Cal laughed. In a tone of controlled anger Jack said, "I'm hearing from you that somehow this is *my* problem, that I just shouldn't be upset about the noise."

Although initially they teased Jack, members stopped joking when they saw that Jack felt hurt. In this particular case, Jack convinced them that soundproofing wasn't a trivial matter and was something they all should care about.

Jack also got points for making organizational *mistakes.* For example:

> At a practitioner meeting, Jack was looking for a sheet that had financial details of Sarah's proposal to get paid for taking medical histories on the phone and seeing the client at Renewal. Jack said, "Let me get that sheet she gave me." He looked through the files in his briefcase and couldn't find it. He was becoming exasperated. Karen and Ron started to laugh. Harry said, "Is this on the agenda?" We laughed. Jack was getting upset and said, "Just a minute."

He went into the office next to the meeting room to look for the sheet. Karen said to the others, "*I love seeing him be human.*" A few minutes later Karen went into the office to help Jack search for the sheet. She found it and brought it into the meeting room, grinning. Jack said, grinning back, "Oh, where did you hide, I mean find, the sheet?" (my emphasis)

In this instance, Jack reinforced his identity as competent not only by getting upset about thinking he had lost the sheet, but by suggesting (in a joking way) that if the sheet were missing, surely someone must have stolen it. After all, Jack was not someone who would lose important documents. Making a mistake humanized him in others' eyes and thus increased his personal authority. And recall, from earlier in this chapter, that Jack at times made jokes that showed some role distance from conventional legitimacy.

For a long time Jack could do no wrong. Whether he was a stickler about procedures or messed up a procedure, whether others teased him or disagreed with him, his "transgressions" seemed to endear him further to others. Jack couldn't lose because he personified members' ideals. He was, to them, a sensitive, yet organizationally competent, man. He could talk about his feelings (see next chapter) as well as he talked about organizational policy.

Gender, Position, and Esteem

Participants at Renewal esteemed some members more than others. Most participants looked up to the practitioners as the professionals of the organization while largely taking staff members for granted (see chapter 5).

But not all practitioners were treated alike. Members treated the male practitioners better than they treated the female practitioners. The female practitioners got more respect than the staff women, but they didn't get the kind of reverence offered to the male practitioners.

Didn't the female practitioners bring some professional legitimacy to Renewal? What was it about the male practitioners that made them, but not the women, candidates for awe? Only the male practitioners could satisfy members' desire to believe they were a legitimate alternative. Why? First, being male became a source of conventional legitimacy for Renewal. Although many women had entered the professions by the time I started this study, members knew that in this society a "real" professional is male.

Second, males were a better resource for building members' *alternative* identity. Professional men have privileges in society at large, such as money, prestige, and authority. Members thought that male practitioners, like other white, middle-class men, could have become conventional healers and enjoyed those privileges. Thus, members saw the male practitioners as those who had given up class privileges for the sake of holistic health and alternative ideals. As others saw it, these men had made heroic sacrifices and thus were the most worthy of the alternative moral identity. Having moral exemplars buttressed members' belief in Renewal as a true alternative, which in turn made members feel good about being a part of it.

Because "real professionals" are (white, middle-class) men, the female practitioners couldn't provide members with the same kind of conventional legitimacy as their male counterparts. At the same time, the female practitioners weren't useful for building members' alternative identity. Why? Women, even if white and middle-class, aren't born with the right to a prestigious career and a high salary. Hence, members didn't think of the female practitioners as having *given up* conventional opportunities in order to pursue an alternative career in holistic health. Because members didn't see these women as having sacrificed conventional legitimacy, the female practitioners couldn't achieve a heroic status.

In fact, the female practitioners, by occupying the conventionally male position of practitioner, raised others' suspicions. Because core members thought of class privilege as something they had proudly rejected, they viewed a woman who chose to be a practitioner as someone who had *sought* privilege. Although her therapy was alternative, she was still someone who had earned credentials and built a practice. In my interviews, a few members described the female practitioners as "masculine." The female practitioners seemed no more masculine to me than the male practitioners. But as those who had taken on a more conventionally masculine position, the women had to prove that they hadn't lost their femininity.

The male practitioners, on the other hand, were assumed to

be atypical male professionals, and thus genuinely alternative, simply by practicing at Renewal. Unless they, like Manny, put the whole enterprise into question, others assumed they had good intentions. Hence, although alternative behaviors—talking about relationships, expressing vulnerability—are considered "womanly" in our culture, the female practitioners *lost* points for their gender. Since members defined an alternative person as someone who had sacrificed conventional legitimacy, women, regardless of how they acted, couldn't become moral exemplars for this alternative organization.

We can also see differences in members' treatment of males and females with credentials by comparing their reactions to Alicia and Frank. Alicia's credentials, two postgraduate degrees, initially made board members suspicious. Even after she was hired, board members who hadn't been on the Personnel Committee wanted to know more about her. Recall that others calmed down after they were told that she cooked and sewed. Since her degrees and work experience masculinized her, thus making her suspect as an alternative person, members found her more acceptable when assured that she had traditionally feminine skills.

But nothing Alicia did could make her extra special. Even her willingness to work for a low salary, and to work for free for the first two months, only made her credentials more palatable. Members still didn't define her decision as a sacrifice.

In the case of Frank, the physician, members *assumed* he was alternative. Any male physician who was willing to join the board and practice a few hours a week at Renewal was beyond suspicion. When he missed his first board meeting to run in the marathon, members glowed; they gave him extra points.

I found gender differences among those who had less involvement in Renewal. Here I'm referring to the male community board members and the community women who did temporary work for Renewal. As I pointed out earlier, the community board members—all of them male—had jobs that gave them conventional legitimacy during the day. As males with successful careers, they didn't need conventional points from their association with Renewal. Rather, they wanted Renewal to help them feel they hadn't relinquished who they'd been in the sixties. Consequently, they argued against some of the conventional aspects of Renewal and pushed for an alternative focus.

The community women who worked intermittently for Renewal—the fund-raiser, MBA student, Chair of the Personnel Committee, and temporary Director—had a distinctly practical orientation. Why was their outlook so different from the male community board members'? Unlike the men, these women *lacked* conventional legitimacy because of their gender and because of their insecure professional status. The women took conventional skills that the outside world hadn't yet given them much credit for, and wanted to try them out in an alternative organization. They wanted to prove their skills by getting things done. Renewal was supposed to provide a friendly place that would honor their conventional skills as well as appreciate their free labor. The women wanted to feel efficacious without giving up their sixties selves.

How did the core members differ from both the men and the women who were less involved? The male community board members and the core members wanted to shore up their alternative identity. But core members also relied on Renewal for conventional legitimacy, something the male community board members didn't need. Hence, unlike the male community board members, core members wanted to retain many bureaucratic signs.

The community women felt good about working for an alternative organization, but, unlike the core members, they weren't *anchored to* the alternative identity. These women were trying to build the conventional legitimacy they lacked and saw nothing wrong with stating their desires for a solvent, efficient, prestigious organization. But core members, whose moral identity was grounded in their belief that they had sacrificed conventional rewards, couldn't accept the community women's proposals. Doing so would have revealed core members' *own* concern with legitimacy. Not surprisingly, the community women stopped participating in Renewal, feeling that others hadn't appreciated their efforts.

Participants found it hard to criticize the male community board members' reactions or suggestions. As men who, despite their conventional achievements, associated themselves with an alternative organization, these board members fit into the categories that participants valued. The community board members usually pushed for more alternative solutions to problems. This threatened the core members; they didn't want to go along with these proposals, yet they still wanted to see themselves as those who upheld alternative ideals. But because the community board members' participation was minimal, core members didn't feel as influenced by them as the male practitioners. Rather than criticizing their suggestions (as they did in the case of the community women), members either paid lip service to what they said or tried to change the subject. These men, too, didn't stay on the board for long.

Although they would have said otherwise, core members wanted community board members and consultants for the legitimacy they provided, not for the work they did. Core members needed some people from the community to fill up the remaining seats on the board. Having male professionals in those slots served members' legitimacy needs well. Core members also liked having consultants because this made them feel they were being responsible organizational actors. (Members might have preferred male consultants, but women formed the available pool.)

The community board members—both women and men—didn't understand that their real job was to prop up the legitimacy of Renewal rather than to change things. But members of both groups, and the community women in particular, worked hard, perhaps too hard for core members' purposes. Both groups challenged core members in ways that threatened to expose the contradiction in their identity.

My function, too, was symbolic, not practical. My name always appeared in the minutes, and core members remarked at my excellent attendance record. Yet no one ever asked me what I was finding out. Although I felt guilty for failing to give them feedback after a long period of time, I don't think they cared. I became a sign of their reality as an organization—the sociologist who faithfully attended meetings and retreats and dutifully took notes. I, like the minutes, became a sign of organizational legitimacy.

four

ALTERNATIVE RITUALS

AT THE START OF BOARD MEETINGS PARTICIPANTS SAT IN A circle, held hands, closed their eyes, and relaxed through deep breathing. At every meeting, retreat, or get-together they greeted one another, and me, with full body hugs that lasted longer than any hugs I'd experienced with people I didn't know well. Meetings typically started fifteen or twenty minutes late because members hugged and chatted as they arrived. And participants showed their appreciation for the time, effort, and goodwill each person gave to Renewal by offering thanks occasionally at meetings and often at retreats.

Participating in these rituals almost always led members to feel they cared about each other. I too enjoyed the good feelings that came out of participating in circles, sharing hugs, and receiving thanks. I didn't, and still don't, doubt the sincerity of those who participated. But, as I will show in the first part of this chapter, these solidarity-producing rituals made it difficult for participants to recognize the unequal treatment they gave each other *outside* these encounters.

Participants engaged in other rituals that focused on conflicts among them. At their day-long retreats members prodded each other to admit pent-up resentments they felt toward others. The group then used its collective wisdom to try to resolve the conflict. I found members' talk and displays of emotion genuine and at times heart wrenching. And their group processing sessions sometimes proved effective: I occasionally saw members resolve interpersonal conflicts or at least learn to live with people with whom they differed.

But what did these rituals do for those who had less power in the organization? Since participants were supposed to air their resentments and hostilities at retreats, I expected members to confront the inequalities between the staff and practitioners. But this never happened. Why? Participants understood interpersonal conflict as originating in the individual psyche or personality. From this view, roles—such as practitioner and staff member—are superficial masks that hide the "real" individual underneath. To them, talking about conflict as relating to power or role relations rather than personality clashes between individuals was irrelevant or even dishonest, for it meant that the individual was hiding behind the social mask. Hence, although members were good at recognizing their own feelings and the feelings of others, their *interpretation* of those feelings was almost always psychological. By personalizing conflicts they also depoliticized them.

Members' rituals also satisfied their identity needs. By participating in circles and retreats, members felt that Renewal was a true alternative. As Karen, a practitioner, put it at a retreat, "We're creating something new here. I mean, how often in regular establishments do people do *group processing*?"

I'll now examine members' rituals in more detail to show how they helped maintain inequalities between the practitioners and the staff.

APPRECIATION CEREMONIES

Circles

What was a circle? Members sat on the floor, moving themselves roughly into the shape of a circle. As they held hands, with their eyes closed, they began to concentrate on their breathing. As in meditation or yoga, some breathed in silence, while others let you hear their breath as it moved slowly and deeply, in and out. The circle was the main solidarity-building ritual at Renewal. Members believed that during circles "good energy" traveled from each person to the next, thus producing a strong collective energy for the whole. After about five minutes, people squeezed hands, smiled at each other and especially at the two people they had held hands with, and then unclasped their hands.

The circle is a widespread symbol for spiritual unity (Campbell 1988). For members, too, circles had a mystical and intimate quality. The touching and deep breathing induced a relaxed, hypnotic state. Since members produced that state *together*, it makes sense that circles produced strong feelings of solidarity among them. Importantly for my analysis, circles also had an equalizing effect on members. The circle is round, symbolizing a continuous, mutual connection. In the circle, no one leads and no one follows; each person has a special, unique "energy" that contributes to the whole.

Members took the symbolism of the circle seriously. They went out of their way to approximate the shape of a circle, even when the space was crowded. Before I knew better, I sat on a chair instead of on the floor when the room was crowded. I felt more like an outsider when I did so, even though I held hands with participants and knew how to do the deep breathing. Literally being above the group felt wrong. Members crouched in uncomfortable positions in front of chairs rather than sitting "loftily" in them.

The ritual required particular skills. You had to know how to breathe the right way, something most members had learned before they joined Renewal. And you had to know when it was time to bring the circle to a close, something you learned by coming to meetings. Knowing when to end the circle was difficult at first, for the hypnotic state alters your sense of time. Members didn't teach each other how to participate; perhaps giving lessons would have demystified the circle. Those who didn't know the breathing method had to learn it elsewhere. For example, I learned the method at a yoga class I took outside Renewal.

Circles became a problem for members when the uninitiated attended meetings. These occasions allowed me to see the constructed nature of circles. For example, at a board meeting, the following occurred:

The room was crowded because of all the guests. Jack said, "Let's begin with a circle." This was the most crowded circle I had observed. It almost looked comical to see people holding hands in a squished circle, especially since part of the understanding is that the energy is supposed to flow throughout the linked hands. Karen's dog started to lick Jack's hand. A few people who noticed began to laugh. Jack said to no one in particular, "Have you ever been licked in a circle before?" (No one ever spoke during circles.) Bob, who was sitting quite far away from Jack said, "No, but I can feel it over here." A few people laughed. This is the first time during my observations that people didn't seem to know when to break the circle. Some people were obviously ready to begin the meeting, others still had their eyes closed. Jack finally said, softly, "Let's begin with business."

This circle didn't have the trancelike quality of other circles, but it nevertheless produced solidarity among core members. They knew that their circles worked when guests were absent. Hence, the presence of guests indirectly reinforced feelings of specialness among core members.

Only once did I see a circle of core members fail. At one poorly attended meeting, members didn't have a quorum (a rare occurrence). The circle was brief, members' nods and smiles looked strained, and we didn't squeeze each others' hands. That's when I realized that squeezing others' hands did more than signal the end of the circle. The equivalent of a hug, it suggested that members felt good about each other and that the circle had been a success. Members felt disheartened that so few people had made it to the meeting. With their spirits low, they didn't feel up for a circle.

Most of the time, members' circles generated genuine feelings of unity. But these good feelings also masked internal divisions. In the context of the ritual, differences in status, income, and authority became irrelevant. Even outside the circle, members believed that social status is superficial, something external to the inner self and thus of no consequence. The circle became an enactment of members' belief that each individual is equally special "underneath it all" and that one's special self can best be realized in communion with others. Members, then, *assumed* that equality existed among them. As inequalities melted in the glow of the circle, members felt that their assumption was right. As a status leveler, circles allowed those with less power and influence to feel they were equal to others where it counted: in their "core self." And those with greater influence and power became "just like everyone else" rather than leaders.

Members held a circle before almost every board meeting (I will analyze the exceptions shortly). In fact, "circle" was always the first item on the agenda of the board meeting, and the Chair wrote it on the blackboard. Ironically, this alternative ritual became a *formalized* feature of the organization. Members might have thought that bureaucratizing the circle demystified it by making it a routine part of the business meeting. Yet making the circle into an agenda item satisfied members' "opposing ambitions"—building a professional organization that enhanced their alternative moral identity. Having the circle as a formal part of the meeting conferred legitimacy on it. At the same time, members' skills at enacting the circle retained its mystical quality. Hence, putting the circle on the agenda didn't put its authenticity into question.

Just as members used characteristics of bureaucracy as indicators of commitment to the holistic mission (see chapter 3), they used alternative rituals as indicators of organizational seriousness. Understanding this double function of circles helps make sense of members' inability to have a successful circle when they didn't have a quorum. The low attendance threatened participants' sense that they could rightfully think of themselves as a serious enterprise *or* a true alternative.

Staff members showed greater interest in circles than the central practitioners. For example, when Jane, a staff member, arrived late to a board meeting, she asked if they had already had a circle. Lateness was fairly common, but I only heard staff members ask that question. Occasionally, Jane or Carla requested a "closing circle" before Jack adjourned the meeting. Again, I never heard practitioners make that request. Although members rarely passed up the opening circle, only Jack and Ron suggested that they do so. Jack made that suggestion when members arrived later than usual or when members had a long agenda. For example, at one meeting, before the circle began, Ron said, "OK, let's have a circle. But make it a short one. We have lots of business to do." Another time, Jack was the one to say, "Well, should we have a quick circle, or should we start business?" Carla said they should have the circle. Which they did.

Staff members valued circles for several reasons. First, as I explore further in the next chapter, they joined Renewal to find community and friendship rather than to engage in business. The circle, by producing solidarity, satisfied that need. But the second reason is, I think, the more important one. Given their subordinate position in the organization, staff had a special interest in a ritual that made them feel like valued members of the group. Understandably, staff wanted to participate in a ritual that made them feel like equals with those who had more power and influence. That their need for equality was greater than their need for solidarity was shown in the following example. At the board meeting, morale was high, and others hardly noticed that a circle hadn't occurred. But staff members still wanted one. From my fieldnotes:

> Last night's meeting was animated, much occurred to produce solidarity and optimism. Almost everyone attended, they were enthusiastic about a new committee, members volunteered for a committee that had previously been hard to fill, and one member who had been away for a while recommitted himself to Renewal. Yet there was no circle at either end. In fact there wasn't a clear "end." Jack didn't adjourn the meeting. Rather, members drifted from "meeting talk" to informal talk when it appeared that the meeting had ended. Jane said softly, "We didn't have a circle." As far as I could tell, only I heard her. The others (in twos and threes) were too engaged in their discussions to hear her.

Since the staff cared more about communion than other members, I expected them to balk at the bureaucratizing of circles. Yet staff's view of this was more complicated. Recall that staff members also gave credence to the conventional model (see chapter 3). Like everyone else, they knew that making the circle a permanent item on the agenda meant that it was more important. And having a circle on the agenda came close to guaranteeing that they'd have one at every board meeting. Thus, formalizing the circle was reassuring to the staff.

But how did they feel when Ron or Jack wanted to forego the circle? Jane and Carla, the two main staff women, might have interpreted other members' willingness to pass up the circle as a lack of commitment to alternative practices. Instead they interpreted it as an act of generosity; these members were willing to sacrifice the circle, the joyful part of the board meeting, to work for the cause. When Jane and Carla made requests for a circle, they did so indirectly. They spoke softly, with their heads down. Were they embarrassed? Yes, because instead of seeing themselves as the defenders of alternative rituals, they saw themselves as putting their personal needs (wanting a circle) before the collective need of the group (getting on with business). Wanting this "luxury item" made them seem needy or selfish to others and to themselves.

Other circles occurred during meetings and retreats. Members experienced these as spontaneous, though they became predictable to me as a researcher. Appreciation circles happened when a valued member of the group announced that she or he was leaving the organization. These circles happened often enough for me to refer to them as "quitting ceremonies" in my fieldnotes. But, not everyone who quit merited a circle. The person had to give a good reason for leaving and convince others that she or he regretted leaving and felt sad about it. Members expected those who quit to say that they valued the time they had spent at Renewal, hated to leave, but had other obligations (such as a new career, moving out of town, taking care of their children). From my fieldnotes:

> Barbara said, "I can't believe it's only been three years, it feels much longer." She started to choke up. "I, I didn't come here to cry, that's why I wrote the letter [she had brought with her]." Her eyes filled with tears.

Board members then followed with verbal thanks and a circle. And, early on in my observations, the following occurred after a board member announced that she was quitting:

> Judy said, "My demands at home make it hard for me to come to Monday night meetings. I feel I've got to spend more time with my kids." Carla said, "When I think of all the benefits you've done, well, we wouldn't have survived without them." Ron said, "I really appreciate all you've done. We'll miss you." Judy seemed moved by Ron's com-

ment and said, "Why, thank you, Ron. Thanks a lot, really." Cal said, "I feel we've sailed together." A circle was suddenly formed. Members seemed to instinctively hold hands and breathe deeply together.

Notice that I used the passive voice to describe this event: "A circle was suddenly formed." When I was a newcomer at Renewal, the circle seemed to come from nowhere. It's not surprising that as a researcher who remained a relative outsider, I eventually experienced these circles as routine. But participants continued to experience these circles as spontaneous and moving.

When a person quit abruptly and without regret, no circles took place, although some members offered perfunctory thanks. Margaret sent a letter but did not show up to say good-bye; board members immediately started talking about how to replace her. Members were surprised when Cal, a practitioner and teacher, quit without explanation. I missed the meeting when Cal resigned, but a few participants talked to me about what happened. In the minutes of that meeting I found the following entry:

> Cal announced his resignation from the Board. "I have a lot to do . . . I'm very busy. That's all I have to say." Board wished he could have shared more of his reasons, accepted his resignation, appreciated his long involvement and service.

Rules about how to quit were strong enough to have their violation mentioned in the minutes. Cal knew the rules and that he was violating them. At a retreat held about a month after he quit, I was surprised to see Cal. From my notes:

> When it came his turn to say what he wanted from the retreat, Cal said, "I want to learn to say good-bye in a better way than I did. I want to share affection, and complain with people. I'm shy about doing that. I'm not interested in Renewal as a business, but as a community of people . . . There's a lot I got from being here. The first meeting I attended here was the last meeting of the first set of Directors of Renewal. People were saying what they'd gotten out of the year; they said it had been healing for them. That's when I thought, 'Hey, this is for me.' I liked it when Ron or

Jack would say I had been helpful on this or that committee, at Board meetings. That felt good. I felt frustration at
Renewal not making enough money and my practice not
making enough money. I also wanted to develop my
friendship with Ron and Jack." He said all this quietly and
with endearment in his voice. Others gave him affection-
ate looks and nodded when he spoke.

Because members experienced quitting circles as spontaneous, these circles had an added dose of authenticity. Since most
people seemed sad to leave, their departure reinforced the idea that
the organization was truly a community in which those who
opened their hearts received others' appreciation. This too reinforced the staff members' sense of specialness, because they were
part of this loving community. Those who left in anger often failed
to write a letter or complain in person. Hence, quitting, when it occurred at board meetings, usually produced solidarity rather than
threatening the belief that they were One.

A member could—though rarely did—break solidarity by
challenging the authenticity of a circle. At retreats, a topic I will turn
to shortly, circles often occurred after members had dealt with an
emotionally trying conflict. On two occasions, the facilitator (Arthur) rejected a member's request for a circle. For example:

> Arthur was facilitating the discussion, helping others deal
> with their conflicts with Ron. Someone mentioned that it
> would be a good time for lunch. Debra said, "Let's have a
> closing circle before lunch." Arthur said, "I don't want a
> circle. I think it's a nicey-nicey way to hide conflict." They
> did not have a circle then and continued to discuss their
> problems with Ron for another half hour. Then we had a
> circle and broke for lunch.

Arthur suggested that people can use circles and other shows of affection in manipulative ways. However, since members were focused on what they thought of as interpersonal rather than
structural conflicts, Arthur's challenge didn't upset the status quo.
Rather, he made the two interactants dig deeper into their personality differences. When Arthur said that having a circle meant that
the two people were avoiding "working on" their conflict, he was
suggesting that others didn't want to suffer the discomfort that can

come with facing interpersonal problems. Hence, Arthur's charge that the circle was premature broke solidarity but failed to provoke a discussion of power relationships.

Giving Thanks

Participants made each other feel special by thanking each other for their work, for personal growth, or for talking about or displaying particular emotions. They usually gave each other thank-yous at retreats. At one retreat, someone suggested that they applaud everyone. Each person said something complimentary about someone else, often referring to the "good work" that person does at Renewal. After each compliment, everyone clapped. Even I was included. Jack said, "I want to applaud Sherryl for her patience in putting up with this group." Participants looked pleased at the compliments they received and happy to accept the applause.

Those who revealed feelings the group considered risky— usually fear or anger—often received hugs, nods, and smiles. For example, at one retreat, several members pushed Cal to say what he "really" felt and chided him for using compliments to cover up his angry feelings. As in the case of circles, members could reject someone's appreciation if they thought it was superficial or a way to avoid saying something nasty. At this meeting, Margaret accused Cal of "handing out gold watches" rather than expressing his anger. Note that once Cal expressed some negative feelings, he received warm feedback, even from the person he was angry at. Then, others followed by giving him thanks:

> Ron said, "I want to know how much of your moving away from Renewal has to do with me." Cal said, "Part of me is pissed off. I think you perceive me as an asshole." Ron said, "Finally! You trusted me enough to say that." Ron embraced Cal. The interchange continued for a while. Ron and Cal agreed to be more open with each other in the future. Ron said, "If I say shitty things to you in my house I want you to tell me, 'Hey, that makes me feel lousy.' We can't leave it like this. I want you to tell me." Then, Margaret, Arthur, Carla, and Vicky each said supportive things to Cal. Margaret said, "I feel I know you better, Cal. Thank you for sharing with us. I feel I can trust you more; I couldn't trust your joys until I experienced your pain, too."

Circles and other thanking ceremonies, then, reinforced members' sense that they were part of a valued community in which each person was an equally special human being. Members could challenge solidarity-producing rituals, but they rarely did. No one challenged the authenticity of a circle or thanking ceremony once it had started. Members could abort a circle before it had begun, but this too was rare. And accusing someone of covering up conflict through a circle challenged only that person's degree of comfort in dealing with conflict, not power relations among members.

Group Processing

About every three months, members spent a day together working on what they defined as their interpersonal problems or personality conflicts. Typically, participants worked hard on these matters in the morning, then broke for lunch. In the afternoon, they continued to work on these problems for a while, then turned to such business matters as "prioritizing organizational goals." (Thus, even retreats built their identity as serious organizational actors.) If the retreat was held in someone's house, as it often was, they prepared supper together and partied in the evening.

They always had a facilitator for the group, usually someone who was affiliated with Renewal, but not on the board. Arthur, who facilitated at two retreats, had a background in group and individual counseling and was considered a "friend" of Renewal. Although participants expected some direction from the facilitator, they also expected everyone to help others talk about their problems. Anyone could jump in and state his or her feelings about someone or comment on what someone had said or had failed to say.

Each person presumably had an equal say, but those who had the most experience in counseling—Jack and Manny in particular—made the most comments, got participants' attention more than others, and served almost as cofacilitators. At a board meeting held prior to the first retreat I attended, a few members said they assumed Jack would facilitate the retreat. He made a point of saying that he *shouldn't* facilitate, that he wanted to participate "like everyone else." By relieving himself of an official leadership role, he was communicating his willingness to be as vulnerable to criticism as other participants. Nevertheless, his comments carried the most weight at retreats because others saw him as the person who knew the most about interpersonal relationships.

Group processing typically focused on two people at a time. Participants gave their attention, for an hour or two, to two people who were "having trouble." Processing was often painful for both parties, though usually more for one than the other, and was always intense. Participants often shed tears. Those who helped the individual "process" a problem as well as those who remained quiet became engrossed in the exchange. Those who had little experience with group processing felt uncomfortable at first, whether watching or participating in the encounters. As a field researcher who remained silent during group processing, I often felt like a voyeur, peering into the pain of others' private relations.

What beliefs about emotions did members bring to retreats? How were they supposed to talk about emotions and which emotions "counted"? Members assumed that everyone has "personal issues," such as fearing dependency, that date back to childhood and remain unresolved in adulthood. Those who repress their feelings and remain unaware of their personal issues stunt their personal growth and make a mess of their relations with others. To become aware of their unconscious issues, people need to have contexts where they can become self-aware and change themselves. Members believed that group processing at retreats provided one such context.

Displaying Interest

At a minimum, core members expected each other to attend retreats. Ron (Program Chair) and Jack (Chair of the Board) attended every retreat. In interviews, others told me they found it hard to imagine a retreat (or a board meeting) without them. Karen (a practitioner Ron had trained) was always there. Jane and Carla (the core staff members) showed up until they began to withdraw from Renewal. Other practitioners and several community board members usually showed up.

Members could remain silent at retreats, as long as they looked involved in what was going on. Participants expected each other to look engrossed, not merely interested, during uncomfortable conflicts. If someone looked away from the action, left the room for longer than a bathroom break, or picked up a book and started to leaf through it, others gave them stares or told them their behavior was inappropriate. These side-involvements were rare not only because others condemned them but because members were drawn to the action.

There were two ways to participate more fully at retreats. One was to help the two people working through their conflicts by asking questions or making comments. The other was to deal openly with one's own interpersonal conflicts. Members interpreted greater involvement as strong signs of commitment to alternative ideals. Since the key practitioners participated both ways, their involvement reinforced others' view of them as those "in the know" *and* those who were willing to risk others' criticisms.

Self-disclosure

Members' rules for self-disclosure fit with their idea that all conflict results from personal issues and uncomfortable feelings about oneself or others. They expected the participant to talk in the first person, admit a "negative" feeling (anger or fear), and address that thought or feeling directly to the person he or she had conflicts with. In addition, they usually treated the person's complaint as a "surface issue"—something far less important than what was going on underneath the surface, in the unconscious of each individual.

Given the individualistic ethos at retreats, members rarely challenged each other's authority or brought up inequalities in status at Renewal. As I mentioned earlier, members thought of titles, money, and prestige as superficial matters that mask the "true" individual. What happened on the rare occasion when a staff member found a way to challenge a practitioner, even within the confines of their ideology? At one retreat, Jane, a staff member, said she distrusted the service Sarah offered at Renewal. In this therapy, the practitioner massages the client's body and makes sweeping motions a few inches above the body. Hence, some "massage" occurs without touching the body.

Jane said, "I don't know what to make of your therapy. It seems flaky to me." Arthur, who was facilitating, said, "Sarah, how does that make you feel?" Sarah said, "Well, I immediately intellectualized it. I know it's not flaky because I know the results." Arthur said, "That's all? How do you *feel*? She [Jane] just told you your work is flaky." Sarah said, "It's disappointing." Jack said, "I'm having trouble here. 'It's'? What is 'it'? 'It's' is not personal. What do you mean?" Sarah said, "I sense disappointment." Jane said, "Sense? What do you mean 'sense'?" Lenny said in a teasing, kind voice, "You just don't want to say you *feel*, Sarah. You want to add just one more little word between 'I' and your feelings, so you add 'sense'." A few people laughed. Sarah said, "Okay." She took a deep breath, then paused. "I *feel* hurt." Everyone smiled and clapped their hands.

Members dodged Jane's challenge to Sarah's therapy and instead prodded Sarah to say she felt hurt. Most members felt kindly toward Sarah because they thought it took courage for an older, more conventional woman to interact in an "alternative" way. Although they defined her therapy as unconventional, they thought of Sarah, a nurse in her mid-fifties, as traditional and grandmotherly. Because of her age, clothing, and demeanor, they considered her willingness to hang around with a bunch of ex-hippies as special.

This was one of the few times that a staff member—or anyone else—challenged a practitioner's expertise. By challenging the legitimacy of a practitioner's service, Jane was calling at least one practitioner's status into question. Although members, when pressed, said they believed that *everyone* has the capacity to heal others, they regarded the practitioners as the "real healers" of the organization and thus deserving of more esteem, respect, and resources. Since only the practitioners decided who could practice at Renewal, Jane's problem with Sarah's therapy indirectly challenged all the practitioners' judgment.

As we saw, members concentrated on teaching Sarah how to talk about her feelings rather than dealing with Jane's issue. How could they so easily ignore Jane's potentially threatening remarks? Members' actions make sense if we understand group processing as one of the ways that members fulfilled their identity needs. Participants weren't interested in using retreats to deal with divisions at Renewal; rather, they wanted retreats to make them feel that they constituted a special community, one in which they trusted each other enough to disclose anger, distrust, or hurt and cared enough about each other to endure the pain of personal confrontations. From participants' perspective, they had dealt with the *hard* issue, getting Sarah to admit she felt hurt. Jane's issue—the effectiveness of Sarah's therapy—became the superficial issue that revealed the "deeper" one beneath.

What about Jane? Participants treated her, like Sarah, as someone who needed to examine her feelings rather than get answers to her questions about Sarah's therapy. Jane said that she had gone to Sarah for therapy and it had done nothing for her. Here's what happened:

> Arthur said to Jane, "I don't feel threatened by what Sarah does, do you?" Jane was getting upset, tears were rolling down her cheeks. She said, "Yes, it doesn't fit my perception of reality. It threatens my beliefs. I mean, that you influence someone by not touching them." She paused for a long while. Then she turned to Sarah and said, "I'm afraid that I could be influenced by you. I don't want to lose control." . . . After admitting this, Jane seemed to feel better. Jane said, "Sarah, I love you." Sarah said, "Jane, I love you." They hugged. Arthur said, "Look at that. Sarah's therapy works!" Everyone laughed.

Jane became a "good" participant and thus won others' approval. She began by challenging someone in a position of authority but ended by expressing her own vulnerability. Jane meant what she said in the quote above, but she also had few options for how she could express her feelings, at least if she wanted others to continue to like her. Through this "group work," Jane's original charge, and the potentially threatening questions it raised, disappeared.

"I" and "We"

Members believed that "true" feelings are unique to the individual and stand apart from his or her social location, culture, or role. They also believed individuals should "own"—i.e., take responsibility for—their feelings. Consequently, those who expressed hurt or anger had to use "I," not "we," when they spoke. Talking about *shared* problems of members of a social category was considered a cop-out, a way to avoid facing one's *personal*, uncomfortable feelings. Those who used "we" were sometimes accused of hiding behind the group instead of taking responsibility for how they felt. Other times, members told the person that she or he was inaccurately projecting her or his feelings onto the group. For example, after one member chastised another for using "we," Lenny commented:

> I think that when I first came here I was saying "I" a lot. I wasn't thinking about Renewal as much, so I didn't say "we." But I think one can go too far in the other direction and use Renewal as a protective "we."

The accepted language of group processing—using "I" and not "we"—made talk of social inequalities almost impossible. Interestingly, it was a practitioner, not a staff member, who used "we" to talk about staff-practitioner problems. Karen was a new practitioner, whom others viewed as Ron's apprentice more than as a practitioner in her own right. She had begun as a volunteer at Renewal, and, perhaps as a consequence of that experience, was more sensitive to staff's position than the other practitioners. Here's what happened:

> Karen said, "Carla [staff member], we think you resent us, we really do." Jack [practitioner] jumped in immediately, saying, "What's this 'we'?" Manny [practitioner] said, "Yeah, I don't like that 'we', either." Jack said, "Who says that's my issue with Carla? If that's your issue, Karen, then own it."

But to "own it" meant that Karen would have had to say that she thought Carla resented *her*, Karen, not Karen the practitioner. But that wasn't what Karen thought. To the contrary, Karen thought Carla liked her quite well. Karen dropped the issue. Others, too, were chastised if they referred to someone in their role (e.g., practitioner) and not their personal identity (first name).

At their own meetings, the practitioners sometimes talked about their sense that the staff resented them. There, practitioners had no trouble talking about "staff problems" or "what we [practitioners] want." And I occasionally heard the practitioners refer to "us" and "them" when they talked about the staff. At the retreat, Jack and Manny claimed to have "different" issues with Carla, but I heard Jack and Manny express the same sentiments as Karen at practitioner meetings. Who made and enforced the rules that rendered such talk unacceptable at retreats? Jack and Manny. Because their practices focused on psychological matters, others looked on them as the experts on interaction, feelings, the unconscious, and individual motivation. They controlled the talk and the interpretations of what was said more than others.

In members' minds, meetings of the board and practitioner meetings were front-stage areas in which participants largely focused on collective matters and refrained from discussing internal conflicts. Retreats, on the other hand, represented a backstage area in which they could deal with stickier matters. Yet, in actuality, practitioner meetings served as a backstage arena where members could talk about themselves as a group with interests to protect and thus concerns about subordinates' resentments of them. Karen, as we saw in the example above, had not yet learned that her backstage area as a practitioner was practitioner meetings, not retreats. To the extent that retreats served as a backstage area more generally, it was a safe one, especially for the powerful, rather than a place to confront inequalities.

Members believed that "we-talk" kept individuals from recognizing and dealing with their uncomfortable feelings about each other. At times, they were right. But, by disallowing any talk of "we" during group processing, members failed to recognize that "I-talk" could also serve as a protection—for the privileged. By proscribing the use of "we," members could maintain their belief that interpersonal conflict at Renewal was a matter of individual difficulties rather than inequalities between classes of people. Thus, retreats—the "official" arena for dealing with conflict—made confrontations between staff and practitioners impossible.

That the purpose of retreats was to generate feelings of specialness among members rather than to control internal divisions is shown by members' acceptance of "we" when someone used it to produce solidarity. On occasion, members said, "We love you" to those who disclosed hurt or anger. I heard the following statements often at retreats: "We're a community," "We're trying to do something different here," or "We care about you."

No one challenged others who said "We care about Renewal" or "Everyone here puts Renewal first." And members were allowed to refer to individuals as members of a group if they were giving them thanks. We can see this by returning to the earlier encounter between Jane and Sarah. In the discussion that followed, Sarah pointed out that Jane wasn't a healer "in the traditional sense." Jim, a community board member, said, "What's that? As if *you're* traditional!" Everyone laughed, since most members thought of Sarah's therapy as the least conventional among them. But Sarah's comment, intended as a technical description of what a healer is, led Lenny to articulate the view that healing isn't restricted to the practitioners:

> Lenny said, "We're all healers." Carla replied, "It's important to hear that we're all equal healers. It's important for me to know that. I think that's the basis of Renewal." Lenny said, "Carla, there are times I've talked to you about something and thought about it for days afterwards. You've been my healer. And I'm not just saying it because I know you want to hear it. It's true." Sarah said to Carla, "You've healed me, too. Perhaps we should use the word more, here." Karen said, "I think it's the whole issue of Renewal, people being unappreciated." A lot of thanking, mostly directed at the staff women, followed.

Even in this example, the staff members, Carla and Jane, weren't referred to as staff members, but as individuals who heal others. And this time Karen's remark, in the context of the appreciation that was going on, didn't lead others to accuse her of projecting what *she* saw as Renewal's main problem on to others. To sum up, *members rejected the use of "we" only when someone used it to express a feeling that could have threatened their belief that they were a community of equals.*

Failed Resolutions

Group processing often led to some kind of resolution. The two people hugged, said they felt they had worked through their problem, or committed themselves to working on it in the future. However, some of the rules of this emotion culture made it possible for "processing" to exacerbate conflicts.

Recall that members could accuse others of cutting their conflict short, prematurely hugging or offering praise to each other.

Participants, then, rejected the authenticity of the resolution and instead pushed the two people farther. Or participants strongly suggested that they continue to work on their problems outside the retreat. For example, after two people "made up," Cal said:

> When Patricia [his wife] and I talk things out, the first thing I feel like doing is jumping into bed. But that doesn't mean that you've fixed everything. I think that these things take time. You can't resolve what's going on in this short time. And you probably feel rushed, because you know the hour we're supposed to be staying is almost up. I think the two of you should work on it [after the retreat].

Sometimes two people hugged, a sign that they had resolved their conflict, only to discover that the meaning of the resolution was different for each of them. The person who received the hug felt betrayed if she—always a woman, in my observations—discovered that the hug didn't mean what she thought it meant. She felt her good feelings were based on a misunderstanding or on the other's insincerity. Here are two examples.

Jack and Carla discussed their romantic relationship during group processing. They had been lovers in the past, but hadn't had sex for a few months. In the crowded meeting room at Renewal, Carla said to Jack:

> "Do you want to have a sexual relationship with me?" Jack said, "Yes." They hugged. They kept talking, and it turned out that Carla thought his "yes" meant that he wanted an exclusive relationship. Jack said, "I don't know that I'll mean this [having a relationship] for more than twenty-four hours, or what." Carla turned red with anger and said curtly, "Well, good luck." She shook his hand vigorously.

Jack was the highest-status member of Renewal (founding member, practitioner, Chair of the Board); Carla was a staff member who hadn't been paid in a long time. And, as the encounter at the retreat made clear, she was also more invested in their romantic relationship than Jack.

How did Jack's and Carla's roles at Renewal play a part in the development of their relationship, the problems they had, and the consequences of their breakup for each one's participation in Renewal? Members failed to address these questions, for they saw this relationship as a generic romantic relationship. Since members assumed that they had transcended matters of gender, status, and power, they didn't have to address them.

In an encounter between Ron, a practitioner, and Karen, Ron's apprentice, Arthur (the facilitator) asked Karen, "What do you want?" She said, "A hug." Ron and Karen hugged. From my fieldnotes:

> The hug didn't end the interaction and almost seemed to make things worse. Ron seemed to treat the hug as the end of the problem and indicated that he felt there hadn't been much of a problem to begin with. He said, "I don't feel there's that much to deal with here. I don't feel our conflict is so great." Arthur said, "What do you want, Karen?" Karen said, "I think we should meet and discuss this later." Ron said, "I'll agree to meeting for an hour." Karen said in an angry tone, "An hour? How can we say that it will be done in an hour? If it's two hours or four hours, it's no good? I'd like to meet for however long it takes." Ron said curtly, "I'm sorry. I only want to meet for an hour." Karen started to cry, softly. There was silence in the room.

What had Ron and Karen been talking about? Karen complained that she felt that Ron wasn't following the rules they had established for sharing their room at Renewal. (They had worked out a schedule for using the room at different times.) Their problem, which members treated as a surface matter, was lodged in Karen's and Ron's needs as practitioners and probably was also related to the fact that Ron was the established therapist and Karen's former teacher. But others saw Karen and Ron's problems as stemming from their different psychological makeups and personal styles. In addition, their "processing" revealed that Ron and Karen had unequal investments in their friendship; Karen was more strongly committed to working on their relationship. That Karen was trying to move a relationship of inequality to one of equality—from teacher-apprentice to colleague and friend—didn't come up. Members assumed that they already treated each other equally. Hence, they had no reason to take Karen's complaint at face value. By treating her and Ron at this retreat as equals, i.e., human beings with special qualities and vulnerabilities, they denied the unequal position that each occupied *outside* the retreat. (I will return later to others' interpretations of Ron's behavior.)

Failed resolutions, then, did not bring inequalities to the surface. Carla wasn't happy about Jack's reaction, but she thought of them as having different ideas about what a romantic relationship should be like. Karen felt hurt that Ron wasn't as invested in their friendship as she'd hoped, but she continued to admire him and tried to be friends with him. In both cases, participants thought of these problems as personal rather than political, entirely as products of differences in individual style or individual needs. Their psychologistic analyses of problems in their relationship left them feeling bad, but didn't immediately lead to a recognition of how power played a part in their situations.

Reinforcing Authority through Vulnerability

According to members' ideology, making oneself vulnerable by admitting anger or fear is risky and therefore takes courage. At retreats, someone who showed fear was a hero, not a fool. But members didn't get equal points for admitting their vulnerabilities, nor did they get equal punishment for withholding their feelings. In this section I will show how group processing buttressed the authority of the privileged male practitioners (Ron and Jack) and at times disempowered the staff women.

As I've argued throughout this book, members revered participants whom they thought of as having sacrificed conventional rewards for holistic health. Thus, members saw Ron and Jack, the key male practitioners, as those who had given up their privileges as middle-class men to participate in the risky business of an alternative health center. Retreats gave Ron and Jack opportunities to show that they had given up the self-protection of the masculine role. Participants, and especially staff members, saw them as atypical men, those willing to self-disclose and emote. Retreats, then, gave the most powerful practitioner/board members the opportunity to "soften" their harder, organizational image. Participants didn't want tough, stoic males in positions of power, for this would have violated their alternative ideals. They wanted their (unacknowledged) leaders to share conventional signs of authority—to be male, middle class, credentialled, and organized—but they also wanted them *occasionally* to display vulnerability. As we saw in chapter 3, members felt good when Jack made a small mistake, for that reinforced their view of him as human. At the same time, recognizing his mistake as anomalous also reinforced his identity as "organized," something they relished.

How did Jack humanize his role at retreats? I noted earlier that members expected Jack to facilitate the retreats (given his counseling skills), but he readily gave that role to Arthur. This suggested to members that he was willing to look at his faults, to make himself vulnerable to others. Doing so also gave Jack the *opportunity* to display vulnerability.

Jack exhibited role distance from his more "together," organized self, especially during retreats and at the get-togethers that followed group processing. At parties, Jack acted childlike, using a baby voice in a jokey sort of way. For example, at one party I noticed that Jack sat on Barbara's lap and talked in a childlike way. Barbara was about twenty years older than Jack and half his size, and others referred to her as the mother of Renewal. In this instance, Jack took on the role of a child.

Jack also humanized his role by saying that he feared others' rejection. For example, at one retreat the following occurred:

> Jack said, "When I was on the West Coast [a few weeks earlier, and he missed a board meeting] I had a dream that Renewal had a party and I wasn't invited. Lenny said in a teasing tone, "It was a good party." Everyone laughed.

Admitting his fears and confessing that he wanted to change things about himself made others all the more impressed with him. And teasing him allowed members to believe they didn't treat him with awe.

The case of Ron is more complicated because he often expressed anger rather than fear and clammed up rather than talking about his feelings. Ironically, Ron established his humanity by *violating* members' expectations. Ron sometimes held back his feelings, seemed to be "away" during group processing, and, as we saw earlier, didn't always promise to work on his problems beyond the retreat.

How did participants interpret Ron's behavior? They thought Ron became angry and resisted admitting fear because he was *deeply* vulnerable, more so than the rest of them. If Ron was less afraid, he'd be more willing to open up to the group and receive their acceptance. In practice this meant that members spent a good deal of time at retreats working on Ron's relationships with others. Spending that much time on Ron was itself an indicator of his importance. Yet the difficulties others had with him didn't seem to lessen his authority, either as a practitioner or as a board member. If anything, such discussions endeared him to others who felt they were forcing him to confront "hard issues." They sought to *understand* his resistance—psychologically—and thus didn't blame him for his behavior. And they sympathized with him for being the focus of so much criticism at retreats.

Withholding feelings or refusing to engage in emotion-talk were major transgressions for which others received criticism. But members treated Ron differently. In interviews, members said that Ron was "difficult," but excused his behavior. They felt he was interactionally inept at times, but had good intentions. And they believed his holding back meant that he was failing to act in his own best interest rather than that he was keeping others from controlling him. Even Karen, whom I interviewed after Ron had hurt her feelings at the retreat, said that she cared a great deal about Ron and couldn't imagine Renewal without him.

Others, then, perceived Ron as vulnerable and believed he needed more attention, nurturing, and coaxing than others. To some extent, they treated him as a "special child." But this child status humanized him and thus reinforced his privileged position. His perceived vulnerability led others to give him "extra appreciation," even at board meetings. Members felt he needed special attention and *deserved* it because of all the work he did for Renewal. For example, at the second board meeting I attended, the following occurred:

> The meeting had gone "overtime" and everyone seemed tired. Suddenly, Ron said, "I have something to say. First, I've been sick this past week, sicker than I've been in the last two or three years. I went to this poetry reading and, well, there's a number of things. But I have to say that I think it's time for me to draw back from Renewal. I feel no one knows how much time I've put into Renewal, and I'm

giving and not getting . . . [He listed four committees he'd
be withdrawing from.] I'll still be chairing the Program
Committee through spring." There was silence for about
thirty seconds. People took each other's hands, including
my own, and started to breathe deeply, with their eyes
shut, for about five minutes. Several people thanked Ron
for the work he'd done.

This sounds like a quitting circle, but I found out later that members
didn't see it that way. I learned that Ron had asked for appreciation
several times in the past, and others saw Ron as needing a boost. They
didn't expect him to resign from any central committees and
counted on him to continue having a strong voice at board meetings.
A few days later, I asked a board member for his interpretation of
what had happened. He said, "What I saw was a cry for help. It's
happened before, and it'll happen again. I think what we saw was
Ron's asking for hugs and help." Participants read Ron well. Two
weeks later, at the next board meeting, Ron appeared healthier and
happier and continued to participate as much as he had before. Contrast members' response to Ron's "cry for help" with the responses to
Carla's and Jane's occasional requests for a closing circle at board
meetings. Only Ron received such appreciation at board meetings.
    Ron also received spontaneous thanks more often than
others. If he showed any sign of opening up or of sharing with
others, he received applause, thanks, or hugs. For example, Ron
agreed to run the Program Committee by consensus, rather than
controlling what went on. Members saw Ron's willingness to work
this way as a major shift, a sign that he was becoming more flexible.
At a retreat the following occurred:

Arthur said, "I want to thank you, Ron, for taking the risk.
More important than if the program gets better or worse is
that you were willing to change. You took what was working and were willing to risk the change. I applaud you for
taking the risk." Arthur started to clap his hands, and everyone followed.

    Ron's high status in the organization led others to interpret
his actions in a positive light. To participants, Ron's transgressions
indicated a wound that needed to be healed. Since participants

thought of practitioners as those who give rather than receive help, thinking of Ron as someone in need of help humanized him. Retreats also gave participants the opportunity to "heal the healer" (as one person put it during group processing). Playing practitioner made staff members feel temporarily equal to the practitioners.

Yet staff members as well as the lowest-status practitioner (Karen) bore others' criticism for breaking the rules. For example, during one retreat, Arthur initiated an encounter with Jane. For a while, Jane refused to discuss their relationship. Here's what happened:

> Jack said to Jane, "I feel that what we're doing here is open, like a family, though my family sure wasn't like this. And if we're going to be open I have to say that I resent you being closed." Margaret said to Jane, "I want you to look at how much power you have in staying silent. What are you waiting for? Don't you know that we love you? I love you." Jane seemed moved by Margaret's statement. She then agreed to meet Arthur some other time to discuss their problems in a smaller group (which Arthur had suggested earlier).

Others accused Jane and Carla of "having power" or engaging in "power plays" when they refused to speak. But no one used such labels when Ron became silent. Why?

Participants expected women—those who presumably like talking about their feelings and know how—to easily express their feelings. This expectation is strongest for women who hold low status positions that require a nurturing kind of emotional labor (Hochschild 1983). Hence, participants expected staff members, whose subordinate status was tied to their role as emotional laborers, to act "womanly"—they should readily talk about their fears and do whatever they could to reconcile a relationship. Hence, participants defined a low-status woman who withheld her feelings as someone who knew better and thus was deliberately making trouble. Her action was a "power play," and she was intentionally breaking solidarity. Men aren't supposed to know how to self-disclose. Hence, participants interpreted Ron's resistance as an unconscious act that required their help.

EQUALITY, GENDER, AND ALTERNATIVE RITUALS

Retreats were the special arena where members enacted their alternative identity. They could only have sustained this identity by believing that they gave each other equal respect as they held hands in circles and shed tears during group processing.

Yet participants treated each other *un*equally at retreats. In theory, every participant could talk about his or her feelings and comment on the problems of others. But in practice, the weight others gave the person's comments, the time they spent on a person's problems, and the support they gave to that person depended on his or her gender and occupational status.

Participants privileged the comments of the male practitioners. They made the practitioners' "problems" central at retreats and found ways to feel empathy for them when they broke the rules. Participants gave the staff women little attention. They censured the staff women when they failed to play by the rules.

Shouldn't the staff women have had the upper hand at retreats? Emotions are associated with the feminine and considered the province of women in this culture. At Renewal, members valued emotion-talk, especially talk about fear and sadness. Weren't the staff women those who had the knowledge and skills members desired?

Participants *did* think of the staff women as those who knew about emotions. But that assumption didn't empower them. Because others thought of the women's skills as "natural," the women didn't get any points for displaying them. At times the staff women *lost* points for their emotionality. Women who express vulnerability —especially those in low-status positions—reinforce others' perception of them as weak and nonauthoritative. Since "woman" is already associated with the feminine, a woman who engages in emotion-talk gets a double dose of femininity and thus further delegitimates herself. *Men* who express vulnerability—especially those in high-status positions—appear "human" and caring rather than nonauthoritative. Hence, the value participants placed on traditionally feminine behaviors strengthened the authority of the men but not the women.

Acting womanly at retreats was either nonrewarding or a liability for the staff women. Consequently, they occasionally invoked the *masculine* persona and withheld their feelings. But because participants expected the staff—as women—to know how to talk about their feelings, participants criticized the staff when they withheld their feelings. Why couldn't the staff women recognize the unequal treatment they received at retreats? The individualistic philosophy of Renewal made it hard for the staff women to see themselves as a *class*—a group with shared status, problems, and interests. Such analyses lay outside their individualistic discourse. If they had glimmers of a different, more sociological view, they still couldn't talk about it at retreats. Participants didn't allow each other to use the language of "we" to refer to group divisions, but instead pushed others to use "I" when expressing dissatisfaction. Hence, staff women couldn't have argued for their collective interests at retreats, even if they had wanted to. Others would have accused them of covering up their individual differences.

The staff women eventually developed a less individual and more structural analysis of how others treated them in the organization. This led most of them to leave Renewal. The next chapter reveals changes in the staff women's understanding of their position in the organization.

five

WAKING UP TO INEQUALITY

EACH STAFF WOMAN WAS AT A LOW POINT BEFORE SHE joined Renewal. The women said they felt lonely and isolated; they doubted their abilities and lacked direction. They wanted to make some kind of change in their lives.

For example, Carla, who eventually became Coordinator of Renewal, had this to say when I interviewed her a few years after she broke her ties with Renewal:

> My child was born in '78, so it must have been the fall of '79 when I joined Renewal. When you have a baby it's really like being in isolation. It was for me for a while. It was like being in prison. Because there's so much work to be done, so much involvement, you know, hour after hour after hour. For me it was very difficult, very confining, and my husband was traveling a lot. So most of it was up to me. I think I was just ready to open up, meet new people. I wasn't aware of that then. I was getting my strength back physically and was ready to start doing something at the time.

Jane, too, felt isolated. She had dropped out of two university programs and disliked her current job:

I had been more of a hermit type person before. I had a few close friends, but not many . . . I've never been clear on what I wanted to do for a career or devote my life to.

Debra had moved from another state and, as she put it, "I didn't know what I was going to do with myself." Familiar with holistic therapies, she sought help for a health problem at Renewal. Debra became a client of two of the practitioners, both of whom she liked and found helpful. As a result, she became interested in participating at Renewal.

Carla gave her impressions of how other staff women became involved at Renewal:

With Jane, her marriage was kind of rocky when she started working there . . . And Vicky, in her case it was her job that was getting shaky.

In my interview with Vicky, she added, "The sense of community was real important to me. My four closest friends had moved out of the area, and I felt kind of stranded." And at a retreat, Evelyn said, "I came here for sanity, for not wanting to feel alone. I had lived in a community before, and I wanted that again. I wanted a family, and healing."

Women who doubt themselves and feel lonely can solve their problems in several ways. They can join a support group for newcomers or new mothers, take night classes at the university, or look for a new job. Why did these women come to Renewal? Since they were already familiar with New Age therapies, they translated their loneliness and self-doubts into a need for "healing." The women had been clients of holistic practitioners or had taken classes (at Renewal or elsewhere) on some form of holistic medicine. All of them had read books and magazines on holistic health. Renewal promised a place in which they could learn to feel better about themselves as individuals and find a special community at the same time.

THE EARLY DAYS

At first, the women volunteered at Renewal. They worked in the main office, answering the phone, updating the mailing list, mailing the membership bulletin, and so on. They also volunteered to work at the annual Holistic Therapies Festival. At this popular event, teachers and practitioners offered free workshops on such topics as massage and relaxation exercises. Its success generated good feelings among those who put it together.

Volunteering at Renewal helped the women feel better about themselves. Their tasks—typing, filing, mailing—lacked prestige, but the women thought of the work as significant. The women believed that their work helped others; it brought the messages and practices of holistic healing to the community. Although holistic therapies vary, the basic idea is that modern living makes everyone vulnerable to mental, emotional, and physical "dis-ease." And health, equated with a good life, is something one must work on daily rather than something one achieves once and for all. Thus, the women defined their work as important to everyone and for all time. It makes sense, then, that the women's participation in Renewal enhanced their self-worth. As Carla put it: "It's a very creative job, in a way exciting, with potential challenges. It *is* right on the frontier in a lot of ways." While Jane was Director of Renewal, I asked her how she had felt about volunteering:

> I enjoyed it. Especially being on the Program Committee and working on the Holistic Therapies Festival. I felt that I was doing something *productive* . . . Holistic healing is something I believe in a lot and feel good about. And I feel like I'm contributing something to society, which is important to me.

The women's respect for holistic healing made them feel good about their work. But that respect also put those who *practiced* holistic healing—the practitioners—above those who *supported* it—themselves. Thinking of their office duties and committee work as part of a cause enhanced the status of their work, but that didn't stop the volunteers/staff women from believing that the practitioners' work was more important. After all, the practitioners, especially Ron and Jack, had practices *and* did committee work.

The staff women looked up to the practitioners not only as holistic healers, but also as pioneers—individuals who had had the imagination, organizing skills, and diligence to produce an alternative health organization. Carla was explicit about how she thought

of the practitioners, and herself, at the start of her volunteer days at
Renewal:

> I can remember when I started volunteering, going to
> work on the Holistic Therapies Festival. I went in with
> some trepidation because it all seemed so new to me. They
> all seemed so intelligent and so educated, and I was feeling
> not so good about myself . . . I was intimidated by the
> people at Renewal. They seemed just more like what I
> wanted to be: progressive-minded, intelligent, motivated,
> and creative enough to take the initiative to create this
> place.

Debra's disappointments with physicians over many years led
her to seek help from alternative healers. Before she came to Renewal, she had rejected medicine and adopted a holistic way of
looking at health problems. She too came to respect holistic healers
in general and the practitioners at Renewal in particular:

> I was so disenchanted with doctors and realized that they
> were so busy giving pills . . . And I've always been aware of
> how my head affects my physical self. Like I thought I was
> pregnant at one time, the doctor thought I was pregnant,
> and everything indicated that I was pregnant. It was be-
> cause I was so scared that I was pregnant that I made my-
> self appear, even to the doctor, that I was pregnant. And I'd
> had enough experiences where my head had directly af-
> fected my health. So I guess I was ready to know that
> health is a total thing . . . I went to Karen [at Renewal] for
> massage. She's such an enthusiastic soul and she started
> working on me and I started telling her about some dreams
> I had been having and she said, "Maybe you'd like to talk
> to Manny." And I started getting the picture of these
> people working together and being available for helping
> you collect these things and put 'em together and get
> things straightened out . . . I had this dream and I thought,
> "This [Renewal] is where I'm supposed to be."

Thus, the staff women respected and, in some cases, revered
the practitioners. Holistic healing has a mystical aura, and this qual-

ity made it likely that the staff women/volunteers would think of
the key practitioners as gurus. As Carla put it:

> There was a certain myth, a feeling. Ron and Jack were
> kind of archetypal [she laughed nervously] or something.
> Especially in the beginning, they had that kind of cha-
> risma, that shamanistic quality.

Other women, too, mentioned the word charisma when they
referred to Ron and Jack. As Lisa put it, "Jack is the charismatic
leader and Ron, too." The "shamanistic quality" that Carla alluded
to above continued, for a while, as a source of authority for the
practitioners in their relationships with the staff women/volun-
teers.

FEELING APPRECIATED

Volunteering or working at Renewal at first made the women feel
good about themselves. They felt competent as actors in the world
outside their homes and happy about the relationships they were
developing at Renewal. By their accounts, the staff women felt appreciated for the work they did. As Carla put it:

> They [the practitioners] accepted me quite readily, and in
> fact I got a lot of good feedback about who I was and what I
> was doing, and I got a lot of attention, just good feelings.
> That was quite reinforcing to my ego, which was some-
> thing I really needed.

All of the staff women became board members at some point,
which added to their feelings of self-worth. The board, as we have
seen, is the overseeing body of Renewal, and staff members felt flattered when the practitioners encouraged them to "run" and voted
for them. At the time, they seemed not to notice that turnover on
the board was high and members often had problems finding
people to fill the twelve slots.

The staff women began as volunteers, but those who stayed
eventually got jobs at Renewal—a title and some pay. Volunteering
meant that they cared enough about holistic health to work without pay, something that made them feel good about themselves.

But the women also thought that a "real job" was something bigger and better than volunteering. If others were willing to pay them and give them a position, they must be good. The following excerpt from Carla's interview shows how getting a job at Renewal increased her sense of competence. She made links between her inability to fit into "ordinary society" and the boost she felt when she got a job at Renewal:

> After I had volunteered for a few months, they decided to hire someone to do publicity and train volunteers in a paid position. I decided to apply for the job. It was sort of a "Why not?" I didn't really think through what it would imply or what I wanted to do with my future. It was just kinda there and I was ready to do something new and I really was totally in synch with the principles of the group.
>
> I didn't relate well to ordinary society. I had never made a comfortable adjustment to that. I did real well in high school, did all the things I was supposed to do— national merit scholar, first in my class, student council, and all that. Then I went to an Ivy League school for a year and something kind of broke down. It just didn't work anymore. I think there was just no good grounding in me about how society works. So then I got involved with my husband and kind of the arts underculture and was never able to break into just a nice ordinary job, feeling good about the way I functioned in society in general.
>
> I needed healing, I guess, so that's why I got involved in Renewal. Anyway, I decided to apply for the job and go for it. I didn't talk it over with my husband. I decided to just take the bull by the horns and do it. I felt really good when I was accepted, it gave me a lot of good strokes. I jumped into the job of publicity and volunteers coordinator.

Debra talked about applying for the job of physical plant coordinator. She was impressed that four people interviewed her, including two of the practitioners. After proudly listing those who interviewed her, she said:

> I was really excited. I really liked these folks. I sure hoped I'd get the job. The next morning they called to say I had the job and they liked my enthusiasm and thought they

needed someone with my kind of energy. So I went to work there and enjoyed things like putting soundproofing on the doors, finding out they'd never caught on that the garbage man would come to the back yard if you called him—'cause they'd taken the garbage over to a Dempsey dumpster. Just sort of getting the physical plant together. And they were so *grateful*.

Eventually, some of the staff women got important-sounding titles for their positions—moving, for example, from office manager to Coordinator or Director. Although their salaries weren't necessarily higher, getting the position suggested to them that others valued their contributions to Renewal.

The women liked others' direct appreciation of their work, as was given during thanking ceremonies at retreats and occasionally in comments made at Renewal or outside it. The women felt that the "important people" at Renewal—especially Jack and Ron— treated them as important. The staff women still thought of the practitioners' work as more important than their own, but they weren't looking for that kind of equality anyway. They wanted to believe they were *part of* something special. If the practitioners valued their work, and them, the staff women could bask in the reflected glory of the charismatic practitioners. Thus, even when the staff women had positions of responsibility, their self-worth was dependent on the practitioners, but the practitioners' self-worth wasn't dependent on them.

ROMANCE, LOVE, AND COMMUNITY

In addition to ridding the women of their self-doubts about their competence in the "outside world," Renewal also satisfied their longing for close relationships. Some of the staff women developed romantic relationships with one or more practitioners at some point during their stay. At least one of the practitioners became aware—in retrospect—of the importance of these relationships in motivating the women's participation. Ron had this to say: "If I may be crass, there was a direct connection between relationships and the women wanting to be here." He then went on to list who had slept with whom at different points in time.

Ron intimated that the staff women had no "real interest" in holistic health, but were there only because of their romantic involvements with practitioners. Hence his use of the term "crass" to describe what he considered the women's main motivation for participating at Renewal. He didn't seem to understand that Renewal held multiple meanings for the staff women, including the belief that they were working for a good cause. His comments also downplayed the importance of *other* relationships the women developed at Renewal. They made friends there and developed a sense of community. I asked Vicky how her relationships had changed over time:

I feel that it has been a steady growth. I feel that I have become a lot closer than when I came. I didn't really know anyone at all for a while. I guess I felt closer to Carla, who had asked me to volunteer. And just as I was around here, I got to know other people better, and I got close to Jack, and closer to Ron, and because Margaret and Ron were together we became good friends. The relationships have just grown.

Wanting a community, and finding it, made Renewal attractive to Debra:

The fact that I could be a member of this little family was really important to me, because my family is all gone. Well, not gone, but all over the place. And after having been a family member all my life, I suddenly had no family. So this seemed like an ideal family—it still does. I feel like they're my family although not all of us are that close.

Lisa recognized that the core members were so tight that new participants might feel excluded. She said:

I enjoy the family type thing, though I don't like people in the community coming in and feeling excluded or not having an outlet to get involved the way they might want to get involved. I'd prefer a more open organization, and yet now I feel I'm sort of one of the more "in" people in the inbred little family, which is nice. And I have really nice friends, but I do think it has its price.

For the staff women, then, participating at Renewal, whether as a volunteer or as an employee, meant that they were working for a good cause with friends and/or a lover. By doing work that had significance that went beyond the specific tasks themselves, the women felt they were doing good for others, outside Renewal. They believed they had found a community of sentiment—like-minded people with whom they could work hard and have fun.

But community meant even more than this to the staff women. They liked being part of a group whose members valued personal growth and honest relationships. Even after they had quit the organization and viewed the practitioners in a more cynical light, they made a point of talking about the insights they had gained about themselves. Carla said:

> My marriage was breaking up. I was going through a lot of real rapid personal growth and learning a lot and proving myself, pushing myself to the limit. *And Renewal was the context for me*, for a while, I mean, I was getting so much back that I hadn't gotten elsewhere for such a long time. (my emphasis)

After Debra quit, she had this to say:

> I'm really crazy about this group. I think they're the most honest—or want to be the most honest—people I ever met in a group. I've never run across people in my experience who are open to improvement like these folks are. They're willing to look at themselves. And I admire that.

And Jane said:

> Renewal has done wonders for my personal growth. I mean, I was pretty isolated before; I had been more of a hermit type person before. I had a few close friends but not very many. I had to learn how to deal with groups of people, which I have a hard time with. And the idea of the whole person and what does that mean for me, that's still what I'm constantly asking myself. What do I like and what's good for me and what can I do to get it?

To summarize, the staff women entered Renewal from a position of weakness. They lacked interpersonal ties and thought of themselves as drifting or as failures in the public realm. They held a mix of conventional and alternative ideas about the worth of different kinds of work. On the conventional side, they believed that "real jobs," and especially careers, were more valuable than volunteer work. On the alternative side, they lauded the work of those who had built unconventional careers, using their talents to further good causes rather than entering the rat race. The male practitioners embodied this mix of ideals: they were bright men who had not only built practices in holistic therapies but had also put together a center that educated the public. The women's belief in the educational value of Renewal was crucial; it allowed them to see themselves as working for a cause rather than helping the practitioners build their individual practices. Some of the staff women revered the practitioners because they had presumably sacrificed better-paying, conventional, self-interested careers to improve the health of the wider community.

The women saw themselves as those who did support work for Renewal. Thinking of their work as less important than the practitioners' work, the women became grateful for others' appreciation of their "minor work" rather than resentful that they didn't get paid the four dollars an hour they were supposed to receive. They had not joined Renewal to make money, but sought personal growth, others' acceptance, close connections with individuals, and a sense of community. Thus, differences in pay between the practitioners and the staff, differences in who got paid and who did not, differences in who had prestige and who did not, became unimportant. For example, after Carla talked about how she had "grown" at Renewal, she added: "The pay and the structure just didn't matter that much."

Carla and Jane were responsible for paying the bills at Renewal. After they paid the rent or utilities they often had nothing left over to pay themselves. The women didn't mind this situation for quite a long time. Since Renewal symbolized the cause, they felt it more important to keep the organization going than to pay themselves. Believing they were making sacrifices for the cause supported their moral identity.

In addition, the women used the individualistic philosophy to dismiss their first hints of resentment about not getting paid. For example, when I asked Jane how she felt about the backsalary owed her, she said, "Well, sometimes it bothers me. But greed is just my issue." Her words tell us two things. First, she defined wanting to get paid what was owed her as being greedy. Second, she defined the problem as personal rather than organizational. The women's initial lack of concern about money also reflected the material conditions of their lives. They had enough money to live on. They had husbands or ex-husbands who gave them some support. One woman had a job, and another had inherited some money.

Changing Perspective

The staff women eventually came to care about who got paid how much and when, even though the material conditions of their lives remained the same. They began to distrust the practitioners, especially Ron and Jack. Their interviews, as we will see, had a mixture of blame and forgiveness. At certain points, they blamed Ron and Jack for having used them to build their individual practices in the name of the collective cause. At other times, they said the practitioners had had good intentions, but their actions still had bad consequences for the staff. For example, Carla said:

> There was enormous exchange there [at Renewal], and a lot of healing went on, but there's still the fact that they, Ron and Jack I mean, had their private practices there, and anything that promotes Renewal will promote their private practices.

And Debra said:

> I was working my four hours a week that I was supposed to be working. I was also volunteering some. I slowly got to feeling—it took a long time—that there was something askew in the fact that I was helping these people who were earning a living. I was voluntarily doing my time for people who were earning a living.

How did the women's change in perspective come about? Capturing the process is difficult, even for the women themselves. The dual structure of the organization existed before the women joined Renewal. Everyone knew the differences in pay between the practitioners and the staff and differences in how a staff member or practitioner got paid.

How, then, did the staff women/volunteers come to believe that these differences made a difference? I outline the process in the following sections, showing how changes in participants' treatment of them, changes in the quality of their relationships with other members, and changes in their jobs at Renewal played a part in the women's redefinition of their position.

Diminishing Appreciation

Like other new members, the staff women at first received appreciation. But after a while, the staff women felt that others— including the practitioners—took their contributions for granted. Carla's comments suggested that others didn't see the staff's role as central:

> The office workers were the undergirdings . . . And I have to say it, that Renewal just never would have survived without the diligence and the faithfulness of me and Jane. And now Marilyn [current Director].

Carla took a deep breath before she said, "And I have to say it." She had left Renewal a few years earlier, yet she was still convincing herself that her role had been important. She seemed concerned that I'd think she was inflating her role.

Margaret, the outspoken woman who had written the "alternative minutes" (see chapter 3), at first thought the staff women's lack of assertiveness meant that they were ineffectual. Over time, she came to believe that the staff's feminine demeanor, and their contributions, were both valuable and unrecognized by others:

> I was reevaluating various parts of the feminine role that I had rejected, like being nurturant. I was really sensing that Jane and Carla gave a lot in that formative stage [of Renewal], a psychic security that they provided, that they were in that nurturant mode. And that Jack and Ron had been in the infancy of their practices. But all those are *intangibles*. What I would have liked to see happen was an articulation of the intangibles and an appreciation of how powerful they can be. And that never happened.

The following incident highlights the staff's disappointment in others' reactions to their efforts. The newsletter (announcing classes and describing services) had just come out. It was a Saturday morning, and copies of the newsletter were sitting on the porch when members arrived for the retreat. As I approached Renewal, I noticed Sarah, a practitioner, holding a copy of the newsletter. Then Arthur appeared, and Jane. I hadn't yet looked at it:

I asked no one in particular, "Oh, how's the newsletter?" Sarah shook her head, then hung her head down and said, "It's really shoddy. It's just not that good." Arthur was leafing through his copy and said, "This isn't professional at all. Renewal has enough trouble looking professional. Look at all these smudges. It's just poor workmanship." Jane said, "Well, we changed printers. This guy was cheaper and he's in the community and he's black." Arthur looked angry and said, "Cause he's black? Geez." Jane said, "Well, you know Carla was trying to hire a minority." Jane was silent for a few moments, then burst out with, "I've heard enough, damn it!" Arthur said, "Jane, are you taking it personally?" Jane said, "You fuckin' well better believe I'm taking this personally!" Arthur said, "Jane, no one's blaming *you*. Why are you taking this personally?" Jane started to cry. Arthur went over and put his arms around her.

Producing the newsletter was Jane and Carla's favorite task. Like other parts of their job, working on the newsletter was time consuming. But it also allowed them to exercise some autonomy and creativity. Because their self-competence was invested in the newsletter, they especially needed others' appreciation for their work in this area. Lenny was the only person who supported them in this incident:

Ninety percent of the people in the community don't care about printing, won't notice the difference. I feel good about the newsletter. There's a problem of the staff working too hard, which has probably worked into this. That's a main frustration at Renewal, that the staff work too hard. If I had worked on the newsletter I'd take those negative comments personally too, and I'd tell the others to stick it, since I would have worked my ass off on it." Carla said softly, "Yes. I feel tired. I don't think it's so bad, and I don't really feel like going back to the printer to complain."

The staff women had come to Renewal looking in part for a place where they could feel efficacious. Losing others' appreciation of their work made it possible for them to see themselves as receiving less than they gave.

CHANGING RELATIONSHIPS

The staff experienced Renewal as a community of friends—some said a family—rather than as an "organization." They valued their attachment to others, the feeling that they were one with a community of special people. From that perspective, the structure of Renewal was a superficial matter, something necessary for the outside world rather than something that had consequences for relationships on the inside.

Without seeing Renewal as an *organization*, it was difficult for the staff women to think of themselves, or the practitioners, as occupying positions in a hierarchy. Rather, they saw themselves as working with friends toward a common goal. Thus, the illusion of equality at Renewal was sustained by the staff women's definition of Renewal as a community and their feelings of attachment to others within it—especially the key practitioners.

Anything that threatened the staff women's sense of community made it possible for them to shift their perception of Renewal from a community to an organization. That shift made it possible, but did not guarantee, that the women could begin to see inequalities between themselves and the practitioners, especially Jack and Ron. For most of the women, this process was slow. As Debra put it earlier, "I slowly got to feeling—it took a long time [to see that] I was voluntarily doing my time for people who were earning a living."

The process was slow because the women enjoyed their relationships with others, especially the core members, for many months. But over time relationships changed. In some cases, the staff women's friends left, leaving big holes to fill. Friends moved out of town, developed other interests, or spent more of their time with their children. In other cases, harmonious relationships turned sour. Despite members' efforts at working on their relationships at retreats or outside Renewal, staff members continued to have problems with some people. The staff women told me they felt angry at some past or current members. For example, when I asked Jane how she felt about those who had left Renewal, I expected her to talk about those she missed. I had, after all, witnessed many "quitting ceremonies" (see chapter 4) by then. She talked mostly about those she found difficult:

> SK: Do you remember how you felt when people quit? I suppose it depends on who.
> Jane: It sure did. Some people I was really relieved about and others I was really sad over. I was sort of sad to see Manny leave. I found Cal hard to deal with. He would tell me something negative that someone had said about me and hurt my feelings and at the same time say, "I'm only telling you this because I'm your friend and I thought you ought to know," and then I'd inquire about it, and nobody else would know about it. So I was wondering, "What's Cal doing this for?" And we'd have these conflicts. He'd have all these brilliant ideas about things that ought to be done around Renewal but not the energy to implement them. And then he would complain that we, the staff, weren't doing our duty because we weren't doing all of his wonderful ideas.

Significantly, Cal, a practitioner, treated Jane as a "staff member," an underling who should execute his ideas rather than as a friend he wanted to work with.

For one woman, a pivotal event led her to shift her perspective. Carla had been involved with Jack, and their relationship came to a dramatic close at a retreat (see chapter 4). The breakup made it possible for Carla to think about the practitioner, her former lover, in a new way, one which not only demystified him but also made him suspect. When I interviewed Carla, she talked about her sudden "awakening" to inequalities at Renewal. Wondering how such epiphanies come about, I asked her what else had been happening around that time:

Well, I was in a relationship with Jack for a while there. But I don't remember the exact correspondence. And that was good in a lot of ways, that was healing and seemed like an honest enough relationship. But it did end. I mean Jack is a person who is just not meant for a committed relationship. That's just his nature. And he has a lot to give, real sincere love to give. But it did make me—I just started to wonder also—well, I was giving a lot to Renewal and I started wondering why he wanted to give me all this that he was giving me. I just was wondering about that.

I wish I could remember the chronology. I think the relationship broke up in January or so, then by February or March I started getting angry and was becoming more aware of everything. *It's possible it was the catalyst, as if the veil were taken away, the rose-colored glasses were taken off.* (my emphasis)

After the breakup, Carla saw Jack as "a practitioner." And she became a "staff member" rather than an intimate of Jack's. Recognizing that one is a staff member doesn't necessarily produce insights into inequality. But Carla, like the other staff women who increasingly saw themselves as occupying a position, *already knew*—but had not cared about—the fact that they made much less money than the practitioners and rarely got paid. Their feelings of separateness made it possible for them to give these facts new meaning. They came to see the benign-sounding division of Renewal into "health services" (practitioners) and "educational services" (staff) as a two-class system.

When the staff had thought of Renewal as a community, they felt comfortable making appointments for the practitioners or talking up the practitioners' services to friends. At that time, signing up someone for a class (in educational services) was no different from making an appointment for a client with a practitioner (health care services). Once they recognized the distinct parts of Renewal as well as their lower position within it, they thought of themselves as supporting the private practices of the practitioners rather than supporting a holistic health community. Earlier, they had seen their contributions to Renewal as gifts; hence, they didn't mind working

for free. Later, they thought of their pay as a salary. Their pay rate—
four dollars an hour—meant that they were underpaid. Their
working without pay became a rip-off. Even the spaces allocated to
practitioners and the staff took on significance. As Carla put it:

> It just seemed so unfair. Here's this office down here [she
> pointed to the floor], and there are the practitioners' of-
> fices up there [she pointed upward]. The two *levels.*

Empty Titles

I mentioned earlier that the women came to feel that participants
didn't appreciate their efforts. But one thing that increased their
feelings of self-worth was the better-sounding job titles they
acquired—such as Coordinator or Director of Renewal. Initially,
this gave them a boost; they believed they'd acquired more responsibilities and authority. And they felt flattered that others thought
them worthy of "better jobs."

But the women found themselves in important-sounding positions without authority. They couldn't hire or fire anyone without
going through the board. In addition, there were still committees,
such as the Personnel Committee, which included members other
than the key staff. This led Carla to refer to the current Director this
way: "She's the—in quotes—Director." And Josh, a community
board member, said:

> J: They [Personnel Committee] were going to make
> sure that the Director had the responsibility, but they [the
> board] didn't want to give the Director all the authority the
> position required; they wanted to retain the authority and
> make certain decisions, like hiring and firing the staff.
> They didn't want the Director to have that power. What
> they wanted was a glorified office manager as Director,
> and a business manager and a treasurer. The board wants
> to be the overseeing, guiding power structure. I think that
> has to change.
>
> SK: You keep saying "they." Who on the board do
> you think has been instrumental in keeping that division
> between responsibility and authority?

J: I think it comes to Jack and Ron, primarily. I think others on the board are real open and willing to give someone a chance and let somebody else do it.

Ironically, the staff women's upward moves in Renewal led them to feel even less appreciated. When the staff women first appeared on the scene, they lacked self-confidence and thus were grateful that the practitioners gave them a chance to prove themselves. Over time, they gained confidence in their abilities and began to feel they *deserved* others' respect and the authority to make important decisions. Recognizing that their titles were empty, they began to feel used by the practitioners as support personnel. Carla put it well:

> It's not like there are private practitioners who are hiring a secretary to take care of their offices. That's not how we got hired. You see, there's that double vision. It *is* hiring a secretary—*in essence*—and yet it's glorified with the name of Director and the fact that Renewal's an alternative organization.

Growing Distrust

The women's distrust of the practitioners grew as they witnessed or took part in discussions ab out expanding services at Renewal. At board meetings, the practitioners resisted hiring practitioners whose services were similar to theirs or using their spaces for special events when they weren't around.

One incident made them especially wary of the practitioners. The staff came up with a way to learn more about holistic healing, give low-cost services to the community, and make some money for the educational part of Renewal. They wanted the practitioners to teach them how to do some body-work (such as foot massages), which they could practice on clients for six dollars an hour, considerably less than clients would pay the practitioners for other services. Staff members were surprised at the practitioners' resistance to their idea. They began to think that the practitioners were threatened by anything that looked like competition and thus were acting out of self-interest rather than the needs of Renewal or the community. The program finally got off the ground, but only after much resistance from the practitioners.

Josh, a community board member, saw things this way:

> I could look around the room [at a board meeting] and see the practitioners react predictably to a suggestion, to a motion or a discussion. And I could see other people thinking, "What are you doing? Why are you saying that? Why can't you see it some other way?" The board members who are not practitioners are not threatened by it, by having the opportunity for this room [main area] to be used every day from nine in the morning until eight at night rather than from one in the afternoon to four in the afternoon.

Margaret also spoke to me about what she called the "possessiveness" of Jack and Ron:

> I thought, these two people [Jack and Ron] with very vested interests were basically manipulating the whole show to do their own things . . . And I think they're very unconscious about the way that they did it, the way they were possessive about Renewal and kept it from really being a *community* center. A lot of group tension involved the mirage that a group was running the thing when in reality Jack and Ron were generating policy.

CONFLICT

Once the staff women saw themselves as working for a low salary for private practitioners, they began to think about money as central to their problems at Renewal. Yet they didn't immediately complain. Why?

First, the staff women, even when I interviewed them after they had quit the organization, felt guilty about having come to care about money. As I argued earlier (see chapter 2), members' moral identity was based in part on their belief that they were *sacrificing* money rather than *making* money. And the staff pointed out to me that the practitioners depended fully on their practices to survive, whereas they had other sources of income.

Second, the women had some sense that others, too, would think of them as selfish for wanting money "Renewal didn't have."

Recall Jane's remark that she cared about not getting paid only because of greed—a personal issue. Since the staff women wrote out the checks for the bills, they, of all people, were expected to know that money was tight.

Third, the women felt uncomfortable thinking of Renewal as a location of class conflict. Such a definition meant that Renewal was an arena of distrust rather than trust, of callousness rather than care. Speaking about injustices in the financial arrangements of Renewal could easily have led the staff women to accuse the practitioners of self-interest and exploitation of those who had less. But the staff women wanted to hold on to the remnants of their trust that Renewal was a solid whole, a special place where people cared about each other. Members found interpersonal conflict at retreats acceptable because it was assumed that they all loved each other and needed only to work on their unresolved psychological problems from childhood. And within their ideology children are innocent and thus can't be blamed for the "issues" they develop and carry with them into adulthood. *A full class analysis would have put their moral identity—their belief in Renewal and themselves as a community of equals—into question.*

Fourth, the women may have hesitated to talk about the issue of money because money itself was not what concerned them. Although the women used the language of "not getting paid" in interviews, this was a gloss for their main concern—that others gave them less respect and appreciation than they thought they deserved. What they learned, in a less-than-conscious way, was that who got paid how much and how often reflected a hierarchy of respect. Thus, for the staff women, money eventually became symbolic of respect, even love.

That the women valued respect and love more than money showed itself in Jane's reaction to the recommendations of the Personnel Committee. Recall from chapter 3 that the committee suggested they hire a full-time Director. Since Jane wanted to work only part-time, this was tantamount to firing her. Jane was much more concerned about losing a low-paying job she rarely got paid for than not receiving pay. As she told me in an interview:

And it just didn't seem that the Personnel Committee was considering the human element in it. That was my feeling.

They based what they were doing on economics, and I don't think that's the value shared by everyone at Renewal. And there were a number of people who didn't think that that was a top priority . . . I felt hurt. I thought, "Oh, these people don't want me."

Near the end of my interview with Margaret, I gave her my hypothesis: that the staff women, when they complained about money, were really complaining about other things. She said:

Yes, yes! Money wasn't a factor for the two main [staff] women, but self-esteem and power came to be. They felt very unappreciated, I think, and very taken for granted. It's almost *because* they were giving it free, you know, that their time and energy could be discounted. 'Cause they were the ladies' auxiliary here.

But some conflict between the staff women and the practitioners did occur, mostly instigated by Carla. The following example shows how a staff woman approached the matter of inequality at Renewal and how the core practitioners responded. Carla went to the practitioner meeting to ask Jack and Sylvia if they'd give Renewal a portion of their income from a special therapy group they were organizing. In the discussion that followed, the practitioners talked about whether this particular group would be "educational." If it were, Jack and Sylvia would have to rent the space in the main area of Renewal, just as any teachers from the outside did. If the therapy group was part of what they regularly did as practitioners, then the rent would be covered by the amount the two individual practitioners already paid for their spaces upstairs. From my fieldnotes:

After about five minutes of discussion about the definition of the therapy group, Carla looked at Jack and said, "It sounds like you're treating this as just a room to hire." Sarah said, "No, I'm hearing that he's so much a part of Renewal that he feels slighted to have to pay." Carla said, "I'm fighting for Renewal. I want to see Renewal on sound financial ground, rather than always just struggling, just making it."

After a few more interchanges, Carla said, "Well, I think there's something wrong about how we're structured when the practitioners get what they get, and Jane and I don't get paid." Sylvia, a new practitioner who had not been active at Renewal in other capacities said, "One thing that really bothered me—I'll say it here—is that people got paid for putting on the Holistic Therapies Festival before the staff got paid." Jack said, "We didn't know at the time that Carla and Jane hadn't gotten paid." Jack looked at Carla and said, "I think you and Jane don't take care of yourselves as well as you might."

Carla turned red, threw her pen down on the floor, and said, angrily, "I'm taking responsibility right now!" Her eyes filled with tears. Jack said, calmly, "But I think you're using it manipulatively. I don't like hearing you say I'm paid more than you when you didn't take care of it before. It was understood that the people who worked on the festival would get less or nothing if staff weren't paid. We were paid soon, so we assumed that you and Jane had been paid." Carla looked shaken. She said softly, "I don't understand. Things have gotten switched around, and now I'm the bad person."

Jack said, "I don't want to blame or be blamed. I just don't want the burden of paying you on Sylvia and me." Sylvia went on to say that she thought it unfair that Carla and Jane don't get paid since they generate business through their secretarial services. Jack said, "I don't know. I have an answering machine at home that works quite well. I get what, maybe three or four calls a week here?"

Carla said, "Well, Jack, what *are* Jane and I doing? What *is* our value?" Jack paused. He spoke haltingly— unusual for him—and softly: "I think it's a large value. And it's not mainly secretarial. You contribute to Renewal in all kinds of important ways."

Lenny added, "I see this happening in small businesses all the time. People have financial trouble so they don't pay themselves. Then they feel they've been cheated. Carla doesn't look at this as a business, so she didn't add up her hours." Carla said, sighing, "I guess that's my mistake, seeing Renewal as a whole." After a few minutes, Jack and Sylvia agreed on what percentage of the money from the special therapy group would go to Renewal.

Carla began her request for money by saying that Renewal needed it. After Jack pushed her a little, she "admitted" that she was bothered by the financial arrangements of Renewal. Instead of dealing with this as a structural problem, Jack psychologized it. He told Carla that she and Jane "don't take care of yourselves as well as you might." His statement also moralized the situation—Carla was blamed for not taking care of herself and was called "manipulative." Later, when Sylvia said that Carla and Jane supported the practitioners through their services, Jack minimized the extent of their help. Carla didn't want others to appreciate her mostly for her secretarial skills, so Jack's comment about the staff's minimal help was less bothersome to her than it might have been. Although Carla could have gotten mad at Jack's assessment of her labor, she instead got to the heart of the matter—*her feeling that the practitioners didn't value her*. She asked questions—"What *are* Jane and I doing? What *is* our value?"—but her accusatory tone made it clear that she already knew the answers, and these answers didn't please her. She got what she had wanted by the end of the encounter—appreciation from the practitioners—but it was too little too late.

Let me turn to another example. For a couple of years, the practitioners and others who worked on particular fund-raisers received a percentage of the money generated by the events. The practitioners often got paid for this work by subtracting the amount owed them from their next month's rent. Community board members turned this policy into an issue; they argued that the practitioners shouldn't be allowed to do this until the staff received the money Renewal owed them. The argument—pushed strongly by the community board members—was that defraying the cost of rent was the same as receiving money, even though the practitioners wouldn't feel the money in their hands.

On one occasion, Ron asked the board to make an exception and have Renewal defray the cost of his rent for the money it owed him. He said, "I'm not questioning the authority of the decision, but for me it's a matter of survival." He implied that the staff women had money apart from Renewal. Carla responded in an angry tone, "I can't afford emotionally not to get paid." No one asked her to say more. Board members, particularly those least involved in Renewal, understood that failing to get paid was an insult and thus emotionally trying. After much discussion, the board rejected Ron's request.

Carla made some attempts to change arrangements at Renewal. She didn't say directly that differences in money and position were tied up with inequalities in respect, nor that Renewal should radically alter patterned inequalities. But she made one specific suggestion for change. Here's what happened:

> Carla had asked to be put on the practitioners' agenda for their meeting. She came to the start of the meeting and said, "I have a need for Renewal to be more participatory, more egalitarian. I think that those who get the most out of Renewal should participate more. And one way to do that is to play a greater part in the nervous system of Renewal, the office. So I'm asking that each of you set a time of about two hours a month when you'll work in the office. I don't want to require it, I'm not saying that, but I think it would be nice if you would commit yourselves this way. I think in terms of Renewal being a whole organism, and I'd like it to be more of that. That means working on all levels, not just as practitioners."
>
> Jack said, "I thought most people here do volunteer work at Renewal." Carla said, "Lenny and Cal do." Cal said, "I have mixed feelings about this. I want to help create the volunteer program and then not do this kind of work at all in the future. I don't want the practitioners to be the fail-safe for the lack of staff." Carla said, "I'd like to see Renewal become more egalitarian, where people work at all levels. I think I've experienced mild resentment, wait, perhaps even more than mild resentment, from people who don't want to deign to do office work. And I think Renewal should be more cooperative."
>
> Jack replied, "I want to support this, but sitting in the office right now doesn't seem attractive to me." Cal added, "I think we could have a few people who work on a Welcome Committee, who welcome people when they first come to Renewal. That might be more attractive to us than

working in the office and is certainly important." Ron said, "I think that's too idealistic. There's hardly enough person power to cover the basic needs, let alone a Welcome Committee." Carla said, "I need you to commit yourselves to a certain time." Manny said, "There's two philosophical issues for me. First there's lack of coverage because of a lack of money. There just isn't enough money to pay someone full time to work in the office, which any business should have. This is a marginal operation, and that's a problem."

Carla replied, "I think it's important that we become solvent. But I've thought about this a lot, especially during my two weeks of vacation, and I think we *also* need new ways to cooperate, to work together. I think that every member of a family should take turns at sweeping the kitchen floor. I just think we need more of a mesh." Karen said, "But not everyone who will sweep the floor will be practicing upstairs. I don't know, Carla. For me, my practice has to come first. I could say I'd do the two hours but if someone calls for an appointment, then I'd give up the other and see the client. It has to be that way, and I resent the fact that you don't think so."

Jack said, "I think there are different ways to be a family. In some families I've been in, people have different roles. Sometimes one person sweeps the floor because that's what they want to do, and other people might be better at doing something else."Ron said, "I'd like to know why you're asking us. If it's because Renewal needs us, then that's OK. I'd rather hear that it's because of that and not a personal thing. If you're insinuating that we don't give at all levels, then I want to know if you're reacting to us as a group, or to certain individuals. Because if this is a personal resentment then you're going to hear a lot of anger from me."

Carla said softly, "I guess this goes back to the time when I was doing a lot of work, there weren't any volunteers; you were getting paid well, and I wasn't getting paid."

Jack said, "Well, what should we do next about

this?" Carla said in a whisper, "Go on to the next agenda item." She got up quickly and left, looking upset.

Jack said, "Let's discuss this next time [in two weeks]. For now, let each person do individually what he or she wants to do." Ron added, "I think we should be very aware of the issue Carla raised and not stuff it under the carpet. I think it's important for the mutual cooperation that the two structures require."

In this encounter, Carla intimated that the practitioners regarded office work—the work she and Jane did—as less important than their own work. She asked the practitioners to work "on all levels, not just as practitioners." Her reference to "levels," a term she also used in her interview, suggested her awareness that members regarded the staff's work as less important than "healing work."

Some of the practitioners said that office work wasn't what they wanted to do. As Jack put it, "sitting in the office right now doesn't seem attractive to me." He made a similar point later, after Carla used the metaphor of the family to talk about members' responsibilities. At that point, Jack said that some family members might prefer sweeping the floor, while others preferred other tasks. Jack implied that all tasks at Renewal are potentially interesting and equally valued by others. These false assumptions allowed him, and most of the other practitioners, to deny their privileged position. They intimated that the staff had *chosen* office work over healing work and that those who did office work received the same rewards as those who did the healing work. But the practitioners' work had more intrinsic value to them than office work had for the staff. And the practitioners received considerably more pay, esteem, respect, and affection from others than the staff women. Also recall that when the staff women tried to change their position by learning and teaching low-level massage skills, the practitioners balked.

Karen's remarks not only denied the subordinate position of the staff women but implied that Carla's request could exploit the practitioners! What was her logic? She offered a quantitative model of work: there is *x* amount of work to be done at Renewal. The practitioners do their share (say, 50 percent), and the staff do their share (say, 50 percent). Carla was asking the practitioners to add two hours a month to their share. This meant that the practitioners would be doing not only their half but also part of the staff's work. Since the staff, as Karen pointed out, wouldn't be doing any of the practitioners' "upstairs" work, the practitioners would be doing more work than the staff. Karen's analysis, like Jack's, omitted inequalities in the *kind* of work staff and practitioners did and the rewards that went with each kind.

The practitioners' responses to Carla allowed them to hold on to their privileged position in the organization without recognizing it as one of privilege. Their reactions made sense within the ideology of Renewal. Members believed that each person has individual gifts and contributes in his or her way to the whole. Hence, someone who worked in the office supposedly received the same rewards, including respect, as someone who practiced holistic healing. The practitioners drew on that ideology—the idea that each person's work is special—and thus denied inequalities between the work of the staff and the work of the practitioners.

Their ideology also enabled Ron to turn Carla's request into a "personal resentment." The practitioners ignored her statement that they benefited more than others from Renewal and instead made statements that assumed each person was treated equally in the organization. Rather than talking about the "two structures"— which Ron mentioned only after Carla left the room—the practitioners treated Carla's statement as a suggestion motivated by personal gain. Carla admitted that she resented not getting paid. Instead of understanding Carla's resentment as a reasonable response to a situation of inequality, they turned it into a "bad intention." Carla left the room, and eventually left Renewal.

TEMPERED RESENTMENT

The staff women didn't develop a completely negative picture of Ron and Jack. Even after the women left Renewal, they had mixed feelings about the practitioners. The staff women's tempered accounts helped them save face; they didn't want to think of themselves as having acted foolishly in the recent past. Since the women felt duped, how did they convince themselves that Jack and Ron were good people?

The staff women's psychological perspective gave them a rhetoric that forgave Ron and Jack even as they criticized them. Recall what went on at retreats. There, most members, including the staff women, interpreted Jack's expressions of vulnerability and Ron's withholding of feelings as indicators of their humanness. Even greed, something the staff women found unacceptable in themselves, seemed understandable in the case of the male practitioners. For example, Carla talked about Jack in a sympathetic tone when she said:

> Jack's insecurity, I think, is reflected in a sense of greed and real resistance to anything that might threaten his livelihood at all. I think he feels a need to create his security out of his practice.

Vicky also talked about Jack's "insecurities."

> V: Jack comes across as being extremely confident and secure, comfortable with what he is doing, knowledgeable in all ways. And after I got to know him as a friend, it was a big shock to find that he had a lot of insecurity, a lot of problems to work out. Was human, in short [she laughed]. Now that I know him as a friend, I see some of those insecurities and stuff come out from time to time on the board. And I see his defensiveness come out.
>
> SK: Like when?
>
> V: Like when we were discussing a new practitioner we're thinking of adding to the staff, someone who does biofeedback. And this is very threatening to Jack because biofeedback deals with stress reduction, and Jack deals with stress reduction. I felt he dealt with it pretty well, knowing how insecure he feels about that. He's afraid his business is going to be taken away and all this . . . He was able to express to the board that he hopes his practice doesn't get smaller, and he doesn't want there to be too much of an overlap. *I thought he was real open to talk about it.* (my emphasis)

But Jack and Ron treated a staff member's "insecurities" about not receiving the money Renewal owed her as needy or selfish. Or she might be told, as Jack told Carla earlier, to take better care of herself. Members supported the practitioners who admitted their insecurities about personal finances, but failed to support those who earned next to nothing and admitted that they wanted to get paid.

In this society, men, especially "professionals," are supposed to define themselves by their achievements, including how much they earn. It's acceptable for a man to worry about competition, although he's not supposed to express that fear publicly. The women admired Jack for "taking a risk" by admitting his fears about money. Women, on the other hand, aren't supposed to define themselves in terms of earnings and other instrumental achievements. By admitting that they resented not getting paid, Carla's and Jane's intentions became suspect.

Members' use of the metaphor of the family to describe Renewal also offered forgiveness. For example, during Debra's interview, she talked about restructuring Renewal "to take the power out of the hands of the few." Later in the same interview she said:

> There's a vestige of the old feelings with Ron and Jack, and I don't blame them. They started this thing. It's like they're a parent and it's really hard to let go of your child and that's sort of where it is now.

And Josh, a community board member who thought the practitioners had too much power, said:

> I don't have any doubt about Ron or Jack's intentions. I have never doubted their vision for Renewal; I have never felt they were overly ego-involved in the process, or any more than others might be—I think more than others are, but I don't think more than others might be . . .
>
> I think the board, especially Ron and Jack, are like the functioning parents, and the staff becomes the babysitter. So the babysitter has to ask the parent if they can do certain things in the house, and every once in a while, they'll say, "Well, now you know what has to be done, you go ahead and take care of it, and we'll be back late tonight. You put the kids to bed, you wash them." After a while, the parents will say, "You can have your friends over for a little while" instead of "No friends, no phone calls." So the par-

ents will loosen up, but it takes a while—takes trust, takes experience, takes time.

When I asked Jane about Ron, she said:

Ron is difficult to deal with at times. But I think he's got a real gift, too, and I think a lot of him. I feel he's real trustworthy underneath it all and part of the family.

The staff women's forgiveness of Jack and Ron was tied to their beliefs about men. The women had a low opinion of men in general. Ironically, their cynicism about men "out there" made it easier for the women to forgive the men in Renewal. They made this comparison and concluded that Jack and Ron were exceptional *men*. These men had chosen unconventional careers and sacrificed privileges along the way; these men engaged in rituals at retreats that put them in a vulnerable position; these men took others' criticisms; these men displayed affection; these men had strong feelings and thus were "deep"; these men talked about how they felt.

Carla's interview captured the staff women's ambivalence toward Jack and Ron. At one point she said:

Ron and Jack would never come right out and say, "We are members of the old society. We are the patriarchs. We are doing something that in this culture gets a lot of money. And we're not gonna be different just because we're in an alternative organization." That's what it *was*, really, but they would never come right out and say that.

But later she added:

I still think Ron and Jack are such wonderful people in many ways. Yet they had such blind spots. Real blind spots. You've got to understand that they are probably better than a lot of men. *They're a lot more human than men on the outside.* (my emphasis)

The staff women, then, forgave the male practitioners and continued to think of them as special men. Yet the staff women were critical of each other—as women. Why? The staff women had a *high* opinion of women in general. Women, they believed, are naturally nurturant and can connect with others easily. The staff women expected even more from women who joined alternative organizations. Ironically, their good feelings about women as a category made it easy for them to find fault with each other.

The women's friendships, like most friendships, had ups and downs. But the women expressed disappointment and sometimes bitterness about their friends at Renewal. For example, Jane had this to say about Carla and Margaret:

> J: We've [Carla and Jane] supposedly been buddy-buddy, but I've felt a lot of competition with her, and I don't feel like I'm a really competitive person unless I feel competitive vibes from someone else. And I usually tend to back out rather than get into a feud. And I mentioned to Carla a few times that I felt some competition going on, and she always says, "Oh, no, I don't think so."
>
> SK: Have you felt like this with others at Renewal?
>
> J: Oh, I've felt competition from various people, mainly women. I think there's a certain level of sexual competition that goes on.
>
> SK: You mean over men?
>
> J: Yeah, attractive men.
>
> SK: Could you elaborate?
>
> J: Well, at the time it was over Jack in a way. Carla was sort of going with Jack, and I felt that any time he made overtures toward me to be friends or go out to lunch I'd feel guilty and hope that Carla wouldn't be mad at me. And I know that when Margaret was on the staff I really found her hard to deal with sometimes, and I don't think I was the only woman to feel that way. A man would walk in and she would become so effusive. And she's very beautiful and witty and outgoing, and I didn't feel I even had a chance to talk to this person. And she wasn't particularly interested in him; she just took over and dominated.

And Debra, who became angry about the inequalities in pay at Renewal, also felt angry at Carla and Jane for not rebelling. As she put it, "I started to get real pissed about it and madder at Carla than at the men."

Instead of developing feelings of solidarity and a united front, the staff women felt jealous, competitive, and angry toward each other. Why? As those who held low-status positions in the organization, the staff women had few opportunities to feel good about themselves. As heterosexual, nonfeminist women, they had one avenue for enhancing their status—getting personal attention from the powerful males. Even the women who had little or no interest in having a sexual relationship with a practitioner used "feminine charm" and flirted with Jack and Ron. Since the practitioners were in a dominant, charismatic position, the women found themselves vying for the men's attention.

The staff women who became interested in having romantic relationships with the practitioners were at a disadvantage. The women thought of good men as scarce. From the women's point of view, the practitioners were potentially ideal partners: these men had both professional prestige and personal sensitivity. Thus, the male practitioners, particularly Ron and Jack, had special value. The practitioners, then, could choose among the women and end one relationship and begin another when they felt like it. In addition, the men had less interest in having a long-term relationship than most of the staff women. Consequently, the women were in an emotionally vulnerable position when a relationship ended. As Vaughan (1990) found in her study of uncoupling, the "initiator" of the leave recovers quicker.

The staff women, then, were in a competitive *situation*. But their individualistic ideology led them to think of their own and other women's jealousy as personal rather than as a product of their unequal position in the organization. A few women talked about sexual competition as natural, a biological given. This account also obscured inequalities between themselves and the male practitioners.

The women didn't only criticize other women. Consistent with their individualistic ideology, their low-status position, and their gender, they also put *themselves* down. For example, Jane accused Margaret of dominating interactions with men, but she also blamed herself for being less attractive and outgoing than Margaret. Debra, after she said she was madder at Carla than the practitioners for the backpay owed the staff, said:

> Carla's caught with all that money that we never paid her, and it looks like she was just turned out to pasture. Now there's some of my own stuff coming out here, 'cause that's

how I feel about my marriage. I was married twenty-three years and was a good wife who was turned out to pasture. So that's really my baggage.

In addition, Debra had some compassion for Carla because she understood her situation. Both had been "put out to pasture."

At times, the women shared feelings of solidarity. But their placement in a situation that left them competing for men made it difficult for them to sustain those feelings. And their apolitical outlook on gender kept them from seeing how their jealousy and competitiveness were linked to gendered inequalities in the organization. Without making that link, collective struggle became impossible. Eventually all the women became disillusioned and left. But they did so one by one.

six
CONCLUSIONS

WHEN I BEGAN THIS STUDY I WAS BOTH LIKE AND UNLIKE
participants at Renewal. Like them, I wanted a better society, one in
which people cared about each other and treated each other with
respect. Unlike them, I suspected that willing it would not make it
so. Things have to be organized in ways that facilitate equality and
care. But how like them I was, especially the practitioners and the
female community board members: I too didn't want to give up
professional privileges. However disguised, board members cared
about credentials and the legitimacy of their workplace. Similarly, I
wanted to become a tenured member of a respected sociology department. Participants at Renewal wanted to think of themselves as
remaining committed to an alternative vision—they hadn't given
up the ideals of the sixties. But they also wanted to find approval for
what they did in the society at large. I too wanted to have it both
ways—study a funky organization and get points for it among academics in my field.

Writing this book and spending fifteen years in academia
have taught me to look more closely at contradictions in the practices of progressive academics and to see which inequalities we
deny, ignore, or hide from. I have also come to see how we repro-

duce gender inequalities in taken-for-granted ways, even if we are ideologically against them. Like people at Renewal, we find creative ways to deny our participation in the maintenance of inequalities. When I began this study, several people were skeptical. They thought of Renewal as a small, flaky organization, one unworthy of study. I too had reservations. But I now see Renewal as a small organization with a big story. What can the patterns found there tell us about inequalities in other groups, organizations, and social movements, especially with regard to gender? And how can we use lessons we learned from Renewal to counter inequalities in conventional arenas as well as in movements for progressive change?

MOVEMENTS

Feminizing Men

At Renewal, members saw themselves as having transcended the divisions created by gender, credentials, and social class. They thought it was enough to believe that all humans are equally special, a belief that would presumably lead them to treat each other equally. But this liberal position ignores the importance of power in relationships. As Victor Seidler (1989:60) put it, "Liberalism has sought to assert that people can be equal as human beings, regardless of the inequalities of social life." But as we saw, social and economic arrangements at Renewal as well as ingrained ideas about gender and credentials led members to treat each other *un*equally.

Changing gender relations wasn't an explicit part of the agenda of participants at Renewal. Could the liberal position members embraced produce greater awareness of gender inequality in a group explicitly oriented toward changing gender roles? Studies indicate that men's groups that seek to humanize "men's roles" also fail to confront gender inequalities. Like Renewal, some men's groups have gatherings where they speak of their individual failings or psychological issues from childhood. But neither the men in these groups nor members of Renewal link these confessions of vulnerability to gender inequalities. Rather, as Paul Lichterman (1989:193) found in his study of Men Against Violence, "members 'processed' [personal feelings] as an end in itself, rather than as a means to accomplishing a new feminist consciousness."

The men at Renewal who displayed their vulnerability upped their status and by doing so *increased* their power with others. Talking about their fears or "personal issues" became a status marker by which others could distinguish them from traditional men. Similarly, Lichterman (1989:191) found that men who participated in group processing validated each other's "status as a changing man" without changing their sexist assumptions or behaviors.

Michael Messner's (1993) characterization of "The New Man" can help us understand the male practitioners at Renewal and the men that Lichterman studied. Messner argues that men want to give up the costs of masculinity but still maintain their power and privilege. The male practitioners at Renewal wanted to have long hair, talk about their fears and hurts, and work in a homey environment. Yet they also wanted to call the shots and have others look up to them as the elite of the organization. Similarly, other "new men" want to cry without censure, talk about their worries, and have more contact with their children. Messner (1993:728) remarks:

> The more general cultural image of The New Man is based almost entirely on the lives of white, middle and upper class, heterosexual men. What we are witnessing is a shift in personal styles and lifestyle of privileged men that eliminate or at least mitigate many of the aspects of "traditional masculinity" that men have found unhealthful or emotionally constraining. At the same time, these shifts . . . do little, if anything, to address the issues of power and inequality raised by feminist women.

Thus, valuing the qualities we conventionally associate with women will not necessarily *empower* women. As Rowena Chapman (1988:248) argues:

> If what we define as female qualities will be highly valued in our brave new future, then to maintain hegemony it is in men's interests to co-opt femininity. In this case, the future may be female but I fear it will still belong to men.

Chapman may be right. Michael Schwalbe (1996) found that members of the mythopoetic men's movement co-opted some practices associated with femininity—for example, crying and admitting fears. Yet the men didn't see themselves as adopting feminine ways. Rather, they redefined these practices as evidence of what they call "deep masculinity."

Some "new men" bring their new sensibilities to their intimate relationships with women. But does a man's ability to talk about his problems with his partner, even problems that might have embarrassed him in the past, empower the woman in the relationship? Sandra Bartky (1990:115) argues that simply by talking about their problems, men are unlikely to shift the balance of power in their relationship:

> In the case of heterosexual intimacy, confession is disempowering not to the man who confesses but to the woman who hears this confession. How so? The woman is not the agent of any institutional power. She has no authority either to exact penance or to interpret the situation according to norms that could, in effect, increase the prestige of the institution she represents, hence her own prestige. Indeed, the exigencies of female tenderness are such as virtually to guarantee the man's absolution by the woman —not on her terms, but on his. Moreover, the man's confession of fear or failure tends to mystify the woman's understanding not only of the power dimension of the relationship between herself and this particular man, but of the relations of power between men and women in general.

Thus, "feminizing" men's behaviors—having men take on some of the practices conventionally assigned to women—can still reproduce gender inequalities.

Political Movements

Members of Renewal would have agreed that most women in the larger society aren't treated as well as men and that staff women in conventional organizations have much less power, prestige, and respect than the professional men they work for. But they also believed that the power differences found in the "outside world" between men and women and between professionals and staff wouldn't matter in *their* organization. They, unlike most people, could leave the baggage of gender and credentials at the front door.

They felt they could "transcend" gender and see each other as "people," human beings of equal value.

Trying to see each other as gender neutral also made them power-blind: they failed to see that the male practitioners received more money, influence, respect, and affection than the female staff members. To members, the differences that counted were those of personality—individual differences that made the self unique. Thus, they failed to see that differences among them were *socially* patterned and mirrored inequalities in the organization.

Participants in the therapeutic movements of the seventies, of which Renewal was a part, cared mostly about individual growth. In contrast, the youth movements that occurred in the sixties— whether against the Vietnam War or universities' investments in South Africa—sought to change the power structure of the society. One might expect people who criticize a society for its sociopolitical inequalities also to reflect on inequalities among *themselves*. Are members of movements oriented to changing society better at dealing with gender inequalities than members of movements that seek individual change?

Whether they seek personal or political change, participants in political movements that lack a feminist agenda either ignore gender or consider it less important than their primary cause. For example, those who participated in the draft resistance movement in the United States were both aware and critical of a political and economic elite that sent those without power off to kill or be killed in Vietnam. Participants in this movement criticized the United States for its bullying of other countries as well as for the class and race inequalities found within its borders. Yet male participants failed to see power differences between the men and the women in their own movement. As Barrie Thorne (1975:191) discovered:

> Women who were active in the Resistance felt confused, ambivalent, frustrated, and increasingly resentful of their position in the movement . . . Full ethical and political self-definition was granted only to men . . . And some Resistance women began to be frustrated by inequalities in daily interaction—the fact, for example, that even if they spoke up in discussions and meetings, they were ignored or patronized.

The goal of the Black Power movement was not only to dismantle the white elite, but to set up a less class-based society. Yet a key participant in the party, Elaine Brown (1992), describes the explicitly sexist acts of men in the movement. In her study of the Left movement in Britain, Cynthia Cockburn (1988:309) found that male participants thought of sexism as something apart from economic inequalities and thus relegated it to a minor place. As she put it: "Even men whose analysis takes in patriarchy do not necessarily see masculinity—and their own part in expressions of masculinity—as a problem that male socialists have to confront in the name of socialism."

And Joni Seager (1993:185–86) found that while participants in the ecology movement recognize that the destruction of the environment makes profits for the corporate elite, they fail to generalize their understanding of power relations to gender:

> Everything seems grist for the mill in the environmental debate over growing pains in the movement. Everything, with one notable exception . . . *gender relations* within the movement. Does it matter that the leadership staff and structure of the environmental establishment in Europe and North America is increasingly male, and white? Does it matter that the leadership structure replicates the structure of the corporations, militaries, and governments that are often their environmental adversaries? Does it matter that, as it "matures," this progressive movement apparently cannot sustain a progressive vision of gender and power relations? Does it matter that the schism in the environmental movement is increasingly between a mostly *male*-led professional elite and a mostly *female*-led grassroots movement?

Understandably, women broke off from some of these movements to form feminist groups, as Barrie Thorne found in her study of the Resistance Movement. Black scholar-activists like bell hooks (1989), Audre Lorde (1984), and Patricia Hill Collins (1991) have made gender inequalities central to antiracist movements. And ecofeminists have formed their own part of the ecology movement.

Perhaps it's naive to ask why men in progressive movements don't generalize their knowledge of inequalities to gender. Those who have power understandably resist giving it up. And men who lack class or race privilege may want to hold on to the one privileged status they have left—being male.

Harry Brod (1989) argues that some men *do* recognize that they have privileges as men. But these men, Brod argues, have an individualistic idea about privilege, believing it is something one can will away by being a good guy. In Brod's words (1989:280–81):

> Privilege is not something I *take*, and which I therefore have the option of *not* taking. It is something that society *gives* me, and unless I change the institutions which give it to me, they will continue to give it, and I will continue to *have* it, however noble and egalitarian my intentions . . . [M]y relative safety in walking the streets, the added authority the timbre of my voice gives what I say, my peace of mind in knowing that however dismal the economy or my personal finances become I will have an advantage in seeking a job, are all aspects of male privilege embedded in social structures, and not subject to my personal renunciation. While men who are pessimistic about the possibilities of social change often express pride in having at least surrendered their own privileges, this attitude reflects a fundamental misunderstanding. To give up male privilege is impossible, to overthrow it is not.

Thus, Brod recognizes the political edge that men have in this society, even men who try to downplay their privileges. He tells us that individuals cannot "surrender their own privileges" but must work together to change the very institutions that give them those privileges.

GENDER CODING

Many signs and objects are culturally coded as masculine or feminine. Pit bulls, pickup trucks, and the color blue are coded masculine; poodles, scooters, and the color pink are coded feminine. Even such seemingly gender-neutral terms as "professional" and "bureaucracy" have masculine connotations. This sort of gender coding is not simply descriptive, but *evaluative*. In a society in which being male is regarded more highly than being female, typifying an object by gender renders it strong or weak, legitimate or illegitimate. In the case of Renewal, the connotative link between maleness and authority was especially important.

The link between maleness and authority is similar to the link between ice and cold. Although these words are not synonymous, it is hard in this culture to think of ice without also thinking of cold. And one can think of other things that are cold besides ice, but coldness can make us think "cold as ice." By analogy, that which is male has authority, though we can also associate authority with other things, such as being white, wealthy, wearing a particular uniform, and so on.

That maleness and authority are linked becomes apparent when that assumption is violated. For instance, visitors to a hospital may assume that the man in white garb is a doctor and be surprised to discover that he is a nurse. The same visitor assumes the woman in white garb is a nurse and is surprised to discover she is a doctor. Everett Hughes (1945) wrote long ago about what he called contradictions of status: we assume that certain statuses go together, e.g., white male physician. And changing one of those statuses, e.g., white female physician, feels wrong. The "contradictions" Hughes referred to have much to do with who we assume is competent and legitimate and who is not.

Given the inequality in status and power between physicians and their patients, it's not surprising that doctors have more interactional control over patients than patients have over doctors. As Candace West (1992) found in her study of doctor-patient interactions, male doctors interrupted their patients far more than patients interrupted their doctors. And doctors "appeared to use interruptions as devices for exercising control over interaction" (1992:301). Yet, in the case of female physicians, she found the reverse: patients interrupted their female doctors "as much or more than these doctors interrupted them" (West 1992: 301–302). That a doctor (someone with authority) is found to be female (someone who lacks it) diminishes or erases the connotation of authority. Patients may thus feel cheated because they haven't gotten the real thing. Only in such female-coded specialties as gynecology and pediatrics are women expected to be doctors. And even here some patients will prefer a male doctor because they assume he will be more competent.

That being male is central to the authority of professionals is shown even more dramatically by Susan Phillips and Margaret Schneider's (1993) recent study of physicians. They found that more than three-quarters of 417 female family practitioners reported that they had experienced sexual harassment by male patients. The "status shield" (Hochschild 1983) provided by professionalism provides little protection when a person with credentials lacks such basic signs of authority as being male. The clients of these physicians did more than disregard the woman's professional authority; they challenged it. Perhaps these men were affronted by a woman's claim to professional authority. By *sexually* harassing her, they reminded her that even if she is a doctor, she is still only a woman.

These studies suggest that it is being male, rather than acting in a masculine fashion, that evokes authority. The woman who holds a position of authority and acts in culturally masculine ways may well be called a "bitch" or an "iron maiden." In a sexist society, she may also be derided as a feminist or a lesbian. Masculinity is an asset only if attached to men. And as I've shown earlier, men in positions of authority who add the right touch of feminine concern get points for doing so. Their feminine behaviors are taken as gifts from the powerful rather than as inappropriately feminine, nonauthoritative behaviors. It matters which body, that of a woman or man, is enacting cultural masculinity or femininity. Acceptance of the man's "gift," however, also depends on *which* feminine behaviors he displays and whether his audience thinks he is gay or straight.

Symbolically, then, "professional" remains a male term, even as women come to occupy professional roles in larger numbers. Since professionals are supposed to know more than their clients, authority is tied up with professionalism. Similarly, a professional organization, as a collective symbol, is coded as masculine while a holistic health center is coded as feminine. This linkage of meanings—maleness and professionalism—may be subtle, even invisible, but it is still powerful. Although no one said it, Renewal, and some of its members' practices (especially their alternative rituals) were understood as feminine. To typify an organization as female or feminine can undermine its seriousness, just as typifying an organization as male or masculine can enhance its status (Acker 1991).

Because of the cultural link between being male and authority, a man can become a prop of authority. At Renewal, which was coded feminine, the male practitioners could become resources for legitimizing this feminine-seeming organization. This was important to members because they wanted to think of Renewal as a professional health center while still maintaining an image of themselves as alternative. The female practitioners, because of their gender, couldn't bring as much authority to Renewal as the male practitioners, although they had more legitimacy than a staff woman (a woman doing women's work). Working for this "feminine" organization couldn't bring legitimacy to the female practitioners and, being female, they couldn't bring as much legitimacy as the male practitioners to Renewal. The male practitioners could do "authority work" for the organization because they were men, and the fact that they could lend legitimacy to Renewal further reinforced their individual authority.

Being male is a central sign of authority, but we expect a cluster of signs to convince us of the legitimacy of a person, group, or organization. Not every man would have had as much authority as the male practitioners at Renewal. Having what members recognized as credentials (an MA degree, a training certificate in a holistic therapy) was also required to gain others' respect. Being male, then, was a necessary, but not sufficient condition for authority. Would a black male or a gay white male have had the same authority at Renewal? I can't be sure, but I doubt that his authority would have been the same as a white, educated, heterosexual male practitioner.

Why? Because Jack and Ron's authority was also buttressed by their relationships with the staff women. These men represented the breadwinners of the organization. The staff women were the housewives of the organization, those who depended on the benevolence of their "husbands." We see this most clearly in Jack and Carla's relationship, when they were a couple. But the staff women who didn't have romantic ties with the male practitioners still responded to them as Renewal's breadwinners/husbands. As the white, male, credentialed, heterosexual men in the organization, they became potential breadwinners. Since these men also acted affectionately toward the staff women and, as Carla put it, were better than men "on the outside," they had a special position—loving husbands.

As Arlie Hochschild (1989:98) found in her study of two-job couples, "only a man can 'do social class' for the family." Similarly, only the male practitioners could "do social class" for Renewal. The female practitioners, by being women, couldn't be the symbolic breadwinners for the organization, no matter how much money they brought in or how good their reputations were as healers.

In a quite different context, Elaine Brown found that being male was necessary for providing authority. Although she was deeply involved in the Black Panther Party and headed it for a while, she found she couldn't live up to the image of a "real" Panther. As she wrote (1992:441), "Nobody said it, but it was understood that the Panther was a man."

Race was also an implicit part of the story at Renewal. As Audre Lorde (in Hurtado 1989:845) wrote, "White women face the pitfall of being seduced into joining the oppressor under the pretense of sharing power. This possibility does not exist in the same way for women of color." The staff women at Renewal, by being white like the male practitioners, had that possibility. And by sharing with the men the idea that individuals can will away inequalities, they were especially vulnerable to the men's "seduction." As Aida Hurtado concluded about the relationship between race, gender, and power:

> white women, as a group, are subordinated through seduction, women of Color, as a group, through rejection. Class position, of course, affects the probability of obtaining the rewards of seduction and the sanctions of rejection. Working-class white women are socialized to believe in the advantage of marrying somebody economically successful, but the probability of obtaining that goal is lower for them than for middle- or upper-class women.

Gender coding can also help explain the attitudes and actions of the female director and some of the community board women who worked on committees at Renewal. These women often seemed the most instrumental and the least "womanly" in their approaches to problems at Renewal. They lacked authority both because of their gender *and* because of their lack of professional status. Having conventional ambitions, they wanted to leave some of their nonauthoritative, womanly traits behind and concentrate on raising their own status and the status of the organization. Unlike the male practitioners, they had no props of authority to sacrifice and were instead trying to *get* some authority. It was in these women's interest to make Renewal into a legitimate place, one that the community wouldn't think of as touchy-feely—a code word for the feminine.

Gender Coding and Social Change

The community board women were concerned primarily with gaining legitimacy and the female practitioners were concerned with maintaining the fragile legitimacy they had gained. Although the two female practitioners at times showed sympathy for the staff women, they had no more interest in radical change than the male practitioners. When Carla suggested that the practitioners do more volunteer work in the office, Karen balked at the suggestion as much as Jack and Ron. The female practitioners resisted Carla's suggestion that members rotate responsibilities or that staff women gain some therapeutic skills. In other words, all the practitioners didn't want to produce a system that would have demystified their practices or abolished a professional elite at Renewal.

Some women in other social movements also take on elements of the dominant culture, with similar conservatizing consequences. These women believe they must increase their legitimacy in the eyes of powerful men in order to bring about change. In their attempts to gain legitimacy, they take on culturally masculine ways of looking and acting that mirror those of the very groups they challenge. For example, Julian Groves (1992) found that participants in the animal rights movement, most of whom were women, played down their compassion for animals in order to appear unemotional and thus rational.

The scientists who did experiments on animals, on the other hand, presented themselves as animal lovers. With the authority of masculine-coded science behind them, the scientists could afford to appear humane. It was hard for the animal rights activists to present themselves as legitimate. The *women's* tears of compassion for the animals or their words of rage about the scientists' actions only made others put them in the category of "crazy women." Yet by masking their feelings they also failed to communicate the values that motivated their movement. They ended up masking compassion and a sense of justice, the very values they'd like to instill not only in scientists but in all citizens.

Similarly, Joni Seager (1993) found in her study of the ecology movement that some leaders worried about appearing too emotional and tried to effect a masculine persona. Yet Seager (1993:189) points out that the masculinizing of the ecology movement, something that has gone along with increasing professionalization, stands in the way of social change:

> For the environmental movement, if "becoming more professional" means making changes to become more credible in the eyes of the existing political and corporate elite . . . then this means that environmentalists must clothe themselves in the same garb of those elites (sometimes literally). If it is assumed that the movement needs to be made more credible to "men in grey suits," it follows that environmentalists must then mirror those men's appearance, language, and ethos. Thus professionalization favors men first, and the "assimilated woman" second— the woman who does not challenge male orthodoxy, the woman who camouflages herself in male language and business clothing, even if she dons this camouflage somewhat cynically and reluctantly.

Women in a variety of movements may convince themselves that taking on men's "appearance, language, and ethos" will make them more convincing to the powerful. But such appearances often coincide with an instrumental rather than a compassionate attitude, as we saw among the community board women at Renewal and the women in the animal rights movement. Taking on the language and ethos of a culture means that one is taking on the frame of reference of the other group—how the powerful ask questions, which questions they consider important, and which kinds of solutions are possible. Women may think of themselves as "playing a game" in the name of a greater good when they don the masculine camouflage, but in doing so they limit themselves to conventional rather than radical approaches to social problems.

CONVENTIONAL ORGANIZATIONS

Humanizing Professional Roles and the Workplace

The story of Renewal can tell us about the possible consequences of adopting practices intended to "humanize" the workplace. In a humanized workplace, workers might occasionally talk about their interactional problems with coworkers or bosses rather than pretend that emotions are irrelevant to the workplace. And such talk might go on at retreats. Participants at Renewal's retreats carried conventional ideas about gender and credentialism into their "alternative rituals." These conventional notions gave more credence to the powerful practitioners than to the powerless staff members. Members of conventional organizations are even more likely to have these ideas. Consequently, the boss who expresses vulnerability at retreats will probably receive more attention—and forgiveness—than the secretary or middle manager.

One way that bosses humanize their workplaces is by referring to the organization as a family. Women should be wary of this label. Renewal's members used that term as a way of telling me that they had close, caring relationships with each other. I found that term apt for a quite different reason: members lived out the gendered roles found in conventional families. In her study of married women's money in the United States from 1870 to 1930, Viviana Zelizer (1989:369) found that "the earmarking of a wife's housekeeping income for collective consumption remained remarkably persistent." And women, she noted, often felt guilty when they used some of the "family money" for personal spending. Similarly, participants at Renewal expected the staff women to forego getting paid in order to keep the organization alive—and to feel good about it.

Women in conventional organizations, especially those that use the "family" rhetoric, might find themselves in conventional gender roles. Like the staff women at Renewal, secretaries in corporations become "office wives" and provide the "human face" of the organization (Kanter 1977; Hochschild 1983). Women in higher positions may find themselves giving, but not getting, nurturance, personal advice, and a shoulder to cry on (Kanter 1977). Others may treat women as big sisters, mothers, or daughters in "the family," roles which deflect from rather than buttress others' belief in their competence. In contrast, men who become "big daddy" or "big brother" win others' approval for showing they care. And the "son" refers to the man the boss or mentor is grooming for a higher position.

In their study of alternative organizations, Joyce Rothschild and Allen Whitt (1986:108) found that practitioners who removed their props of authority signified that they "are human, and accordingly, that their professional judgments are open to question." But my study suggests that professional *men* who lose their prop of authority gain others' trust rather than leaving themselves open to others' challenges. When professional *women* lose their prop of professionalism they don't have their gender as a backup prop, and thus lose complete authority.

Thus, women in high-status positions who humanize their roles may end up with as little, or less, authority than women who display a professional distance. As we saw at Renewal, only the *men* who had a more feminine style got points for it. Women in professional positions are caught in a double bind: if they retain a professional distance, others may accuse them of acting like men and thus giving an inappropriate display of authority. If they act in a personal, egalitarian way with others, they may undermine their own authority.

But this isn't necessarily a tragedy. For professional women who seek to transform the institutions they are a part of, our contradictory position becomes a plus. The person who lives in two worlds can occupy a special position: instead of taking either world for granted, such a person has enough distance to critically analyze both (Stonequist 1961). Feminists have also come to recognize the radical potential of being on the margins (Lorde 1984). Once we realize that we can never fully belong, we might become less invested in playing the game and be able to assess the structure of the organization/institution and the values that underlie it.

LESSONS

At Renewal, members took on a moral identity, one that I called "alternative." They became so invested in the identity as a measure of their worth that they didn't see how they contradicted their own ideals. Similarly, as I pointed out in this chapter, participants in progressive social movements often fail to apply their sociopolitical analyses to themselves.

Participants in progressive social movements may believe, like members of Renewal, that taking on the moral identity of leftist, antiracist, or feminist is enough. Participants may assume that membership in the group guarantees that they have purged themselves of the sexism (or racism, classism, heterosexism) that permeates the society "out there." But as the case of Renewal shows, people cannot will away years of ingrained ideas about who deserves more respect, resources, and affection. Many inequalities may thus be reproduced beneath conscious awareness.

How can members of progressive groups or organizations become aware of their own contradictions? In their study of five radically democratic organizations, Joyce Rothschild and Allen Whitt (1986:84) found that group encounters of "mutual and self-criticism . . . support[ed] the egalitarian and participatory character of collectivist organizations." Unlike retreats at Renewal, members of collectivist organizations focused more on unequal influence and power in the organization than on psychological issues.

Yet even in these organizations, members failed to analyze how social class influenced the balance of power and respect among them. For example, in their interviews with participants, Rothschild and Whitt (1986:97–98) discovered that working-class members felt uncomfortable in these largely middle-class organizations. Significantly, "the private uneasiness of working class members was never publicly acknowledged in the observed organizations" (Rothschild and Whitt 1986:98; see also Swidler 1979, Mansbridge 1980). Thus, even when members of organizations institutionalize democratic practices—e.g., equal pay, rotation of jobs, and group processing—they may still fail to see how the inequalities they reject in the wider society infiltrate their own organization.

What seems to be missing from these organizations is a process that would make members aware of the power and privileges that attach to their identities. At Renewal, members failed to see how organizational positions (staff member, practitioner) and ascribed statuses (man, woman) brought unequal benefits to participants. Rothschild and Whitt's study suggests that members of collectivist organizations try to ensure that people in different jobs get equal respect, but they don't necessarily deal with the "hidden" inequalities of race, class, and gender.

Why is it so hard for members of progressive organizations to face these contradictions? Those who adopt a moral identity claim specialness; members believe the identity confers goodness on them. Sharing that identity with others, whether through marches or through "alternative rituals," also builds solidarity among participants. Feeling good about oneself through an identity that ties one to a community is something that many of us wish for. It's understandable that once we have it, we don't want to take a critical look at ourselves to see if we are "deserving" of the identity.

Making any group face differences of gender, race, or class threatens solidarity. This is because these differences are rarely innocent, but reflect patterns of power and influence. Yet feminists have learned that progressive movement is thwarted if participants don't recognize inequalities among themselves. We have learned through experience how the identity of "sister"—which presumes a sisterhood—becomes a gloss for togetherness that denies differences among women (Lorde 1984).

Acknowledging such differences is painful but also enables us to recognize our own privileges and to see links between our own oppression and the oppression of others. Patricia Hill Collins (1991:220) tells us:

> Although most individuals have little difficulty identifying their own victimization within some major system of oppression—whether it be by race, social class, religion, physical ability, sexual orientation, ethnicity, age, or gender—they typically fail to see how their thoughts and actions uphold someone else's subordination . . . Oppression is filled with such contradictions because these approaches fail to recognize that a matrix of domination contains few pure victims or oppressors. Each individual derives varying amounts of penalty and privilege from the multiple systems of oppression which frame everyone's lives.

Our identities locate us in this "matrix of domination," and without examining the blind spots we develop by adopting one or another identity, we may well reproduce the inequalities we seek to abolish.

When we take on the identity of feminist, leftist, or antiracist we can do one of two things: don the identity and feel good about ourselves for having it, or see it as a symbol of a lifetime commitment to critical self-reflection and radical action. From Renewal I learned that in a society permeated by inequalities, we can't get rid of the patterns of domination and subordination we participate in unless we continually examine our contradictions. And we find these contradictions by tracing out the political implications of our moral identities. Without such self-examination we may think of ourselves as progressive, but fail to build a better alternative.

REFERENCES

Acker, Joan. 1991. "Hierarchies, Jobs, Bodies: A Theory of Gendered Organizations." In *The Social Construction of Gender*, edited by Judith Lorder and
Susan A. Farrell, 162–79. Newbury Park, Calif.: Sage.

Agger, Ben. 1991. "Critical Theory, Poststructuralism, Postmodernism:
Their Sociological Relevance." *Annual Review of Sociology* 17:105–31.

Ball, Donald W. 1970. "An Abortion Clinic Ethnography." In *Qualitative
Methodology*, edited by William J. Filstead, 174–85. Chicago: Rand
McNally.

Bartky, Sandra L. 1990. "Feeding Egos and Tending Wounds: Deference and
Disaffection in Women's Emotional Labor." In *Femininity and Domination:
Studies in the Phenomenology of Oppression*, edited by Sandra L. Bartky, 99–
119. New York: Routledge.

Becker, Howard S. 1970. "The Nature of a Profession." In *Sociological Work:
Method and Substance*, by Howard S. Becker, 87–103. Chicago: Aldine.

Berger, Bennett. 1981. *The Survival of a Counterculture: Ideological Work and
Everyday Life Among Rural Communards*. Berkeley: University of California
Press.

Blumer, Herbert. 1969. *Symbolic Interactionism*. Englewood Cliffs, N.J.:
Prentice-Hall.

Blumstein, Phillip, and Pepper Schwartz. 1983. *American Couples*. New
York: William Morrow.

Brod, Harry. 1989. "Work Clothes and Leisure Suits: The Class Basis and
Bias of the Men's Movement." In *Men's Lives*, edited by Michael S. Kim-
mel and Michael A. Messner, 276–87. New York: Macmillan.

Brown, Elaine. 1992. *A Taste of Power: A Black Woman's Story.* New York: Pantheon Books.

Campbell, Joseph. 1988. *The Power of Myth.* New York: Doubleday.

Case, John, and Rosemary C. R. Taylor, eds. 1979. *Co-ops, Communes and Collectives: Experiments in Social Change in the 1960s and 1970s.* New York: Pantheon Books.

Chapman, Rowena. 1988. "The Great Pretender: Variations on the New Man Theme." In *Male Order: Unwrapping Masculinity,* edited by Rowena Chapman and Jonathan Rutherford, 225–48. London: Lawrence and Wishart.

Cockburn, Cynthia. 1988. "Masculinity, the Left and Feminism." In *Male Order: Unwrapping Masculinity,* edited by Rowena Chapman and Jonathan Rutherford, 303–29. London: Lawrence and Wishart.

Collins, Patricia Hill. 1991. *Black Feminist Thought: Knowledge, Consciousness, and the Politics of Empowerment.* New York: Routledge.

DiMaggio, Paul L., and Walter W. Powell. 1983. "The Iron Cage Revisited: Institutional Isomorphism and Collective Rationality in Organizational Fields." *American Sociological Review* 48:147–60.

Flax, Jane. 1987. "Postmodernism and Gender Relations in Feminist Theory." *Signs* 12: 621–43.

Freeman, Jo. 1972–73. "The Tyranny of Structurelessness." *Berkeley Journal of Sociology* 17:151–64.

Gilligan, Carol. 1982. *In a Different Voice: Psychological Theory and Moral Development.* Cambridge: Harvard University Press.

Goffman, Erving. 1961. *Asylums.* Garden City, N.Y.: Doubleday.

Groves, Julian M. 1992. *Animal Rights and Animal Research: The Social Context of Moral Decisions in Community Conflicts over Science.* Ph.D. diss., University of North Carolina, Chapel Hill.

Hochschild, Arlie R. 1983. *The Managed Heart: Commercialization of Human Feeling.* Berkeley: University of California Press.

———. 1989. "The Economy of Gratitude." In *The Sociology of Emotions: Original Essays and Research Papers,* edited by David D. Franks and E. Doyle McCarthy, 95–113. Greenwich, Conn.: JAI Press.

hooks, bell. 1989. *Talking Back: Thinking Feminist, Thinking Black.* Boston: South End Press.

Hughes, Everett C. 1945. "Dilemmas and Contradictions of Status." *American Journal of Sociology* 50:353–54.

Hurtado, Aida. 1989. "Relating to Privilege: Seduction and Rejection in the Subordination of White Women and Women of Color." *Signs* 14:833–55.

Jaggar, Alison M. 1989. "Love and Knowledge: Emotion in Feminist Epistemology." In *Gender/Body/Knowledge: Feminist Reconstructions of Being and Knowing,* edited by Alison M. Jaggar and Susan R. Bordo, 145–71. New Brunswick, N.J.: Rutgers University Press.

Kanter, Rosabeth M. 1977. *Men and Women of the Corporation.* New York: Basic Books.

Katz, Jack. 1975. "Essences as Moral Identities: Verifiability and Responsibility in Imputations of Deviance and Charisma." *American Journal of Sociology* 80:1369–90.

Kleinman, Sherryl. 1984. *Equals before God: Seminarians as Humanistic Professionals.* Chicago: University of Chicago Press.

Kleinman, Sherryl, and Martha A. Copp. 1993. *Emotions and Fieldwork.* Newbury Park, Calif.: Sage.

Lichterman, Paul. 1989. "Making a Politics of Masculinity." *Comparative Social Research* 11:185–208.

Liebow, Elliott. 1967. *Tally's Corner: A Study of Negro Street Corner Men.* Boston: Little, Brown.

Lofland, John, and Lyn Lofland. 1984. *Analyzing Social Settings: A Guide to Qualitative Observation and Analysis.* Belmont, Calif.: Wadsworth.

Lorde, Audre. 1984. "Age, Race, Class and Sex: Women Redefining Difference." In *Sister Outsider,* by Audre Lorde, 114–23. Freedom, Calif.: Crossing Press.

Mansbridge, Jane J. 1980. *Beyond Adversary Democracy.* New York: Basic Books.

Mead, George H. 1934. *Mind, Self, and Society.* Chicago: University of Chicago Press.

Messner, Michael A. 1993. "'Changing Men' and Feminist Politics in the U.S." *Theory and Society* 22:723–37.

Meyer, John W., and Brian Rowan. 1977. "Institutionalized Organizations: Formal Structure as Myth and Ceremony." *American Journal of Sociology* 83:340–63.

Newman, Katherine S. 1988. *Falling From Grace: The Experience of Downward Mobility in the American Middle Class.* New York: The Free Press.

Olesen, Virginia, and Elvi W. Whittaker. 1968. *The Silent Dialogue.* San Francisco: Jossey-Bass.

Phillips, Susan P., and Margaret S. Schneider. 1993. "Sexual Harassment of Female Doctors by Patients." *New England Journal of Medicine* 329:1936–39.

Reinharz, Shulamit. 1983. "Consulting to the Alternative Work Setting: A Suggested Strategy for Community Psychology." *Journal of Community Psychology* 11:199–212.

Rothschild, Joyce, and J. Allen Whitt. 1986. *The Cooperative Workplace: Potentials and Dilemmas of Organizational Democracy and Participation.* New York: Cambridge University Press.

Schwalbe, Michael L. 1996. *Unlocking the Iron Cage: The Men's Movement, Gender Politics, and American Culture.* New York: Oxford University Press.

Seager, Joni. 1993. *Earth Follies: Coming to Feminist Terms with the Global Environmental Crisis.* New York: Routledge.

Seidler, Victor J. 1989. *Rediscovering Masculinity: Reason, Language, and Sexuality.* London: Routledge.

Sennett, Richard, and Jonathan Cobb. 1972. *The Hidden Injuries of Class.* New York: Random House.

Smith, Allen C. III, and Sherryl Kleinman. 1989. "Managing Emotions in

Medical School: Students' Contacts with the Living and the Dead." *Social Psychology Quarterly* 52:56–69.

Stonequist, E. V. 1961. *The Marginal Man.* New York: Russell and Russell.

Swidler, Ann. 1979. *Organization without Authority: Dilemmas of Social Control in Free Schools.* Cambridge, Mass.: Harvard University Press.

Thomas, Jim. 1993. *Doing Critical Ethnography.* Newbury Park, Calif.: Sage.

Thorne, Barrie. 1975. "Women in the Draft Resistance Movement: A Case Study of Sex Roles and Social Movements." *Sex Roles* 1:179–95.

Vaughan, Diane. 1990. *Uncoupling: Turning Points in Intimate Relationships.* New York: Vintage.

West, Candace. 1992. "When the Doctor Is a 'Lady': Power, Status and Gender in Physician-Patient Encounters," In *Social Psychological Foundations: Readings from the Interactionist Perspective,* edited by Harvey A. Farberman, Gary Alan Fine, and John Johnson, 287–306. Greenwich, Conn.: JAI Press.

Zelizer, Viviana. 1989. "The Social Meaning of Money: 'Special Monies.'" *American Journal of Sociology* 95:342–77.

INDEX